INTELLIGENCE CAME FIRST

QUEST BOOKS

are published by The Theosophical Society
in America, a branch of a world
organization dedicated to the promotion
of brotherhood and the encouragement
of the study of religion, philosophy,
and science, to the end that many may
better understand himself and his
place in the universe. The Society
stands for complete freedom
of individual search and belief. Quest
Books are offered as a contribution to
man's search for truth.

Cover illustration by JANE EVANS

INTELLIGENCE CAME FIRST

Edited by

E. LESTER SMITH, D.Sc., F.R.S.

A QUEST BOOK
Published under a grant from the Kern Foundation

THE THEOSOPHICAL PUBLISHING HOUSE
Wheaton, Ill., U.S.A.
Madras, India / London, England

© The Theosophical Publishing House, 1975

The Theosophical Publishing House, Wheaton, Illinois is
a department of The Theosophical Society in America

First edition, 1975

Smith, Ernest Lester, 1904-
   Intelligence came first.

   (A Quest book)
   1. Mind and body.   I. Title.
BF161.S58   153.7   74-19053
ISBN 0-8356-0458-6
ISBN 0-8356-0456-X pbk.

PRINTED IN THE UNITED STATES OF AMERICA

Today there is a wide measure of agreement, which on the physical side of science approaches almost to unanimity, that the stream of knowledge is heading towards a nonmechanical reality; the universe begins to look more like a great thought than like a great machine.

Mind no longer appears as an accidental intruder into the realm of matter; we are beginning to suspect that we ought rather to hail it as the creator and governor of the realm of matter.

Sir James Jeans, F.R.S.
The Mysterious Universe

CONTENTS

DIAGRAMS

FOREWORD

This book has been produced by a group of well qualified individuals who have a scientific approach to the subject. Most of the material was drafted by the Editor, parts by other members of the group. At our monthly meetings, every chapter in turn was read and discussed, then redrafted by the Editor and discussed again at later meetings. After further revision the manuscript was circulated for final amendments and approval. Accordingly, members of the group who took part in these discussions are regarded as contributors even if they did not write any of the original drafts.

Grateful thanks for typing and retyping chapters are due to Miss Winifred Marshall and Mrs. June Feldon.

Contributors

Dr. H. Tudor Edmunds, M.B., B.S., M.R.C.S., L.R.C.P.
Professor Arthur J. Ellison, D.Sc. (Eng.), C.Eng., F.I.Mech.E., F.I.E.E., Sen.Mem.I.E.E.E.
Mrs. Marion E. Ellison
Forbes G. Perry, C.Eng., M.I.Mech.E., A.F.R.Ae.S.
V. Wallace Slater, B.Sc., F.R.I.C., M.I.Chem.E.
E. Lester Smith, D.Sc., F.R.I.C., F.R.S.
Miss Corona G. Trew, Ph.D., D.Sc.
K.B. Wakelam B.Sc.

INTRODUCTION

This book starts from the premise that consciousness is a fact of nature, since it is a universal human experience. Consciousness of some kind must presumably be extended to other natural orders as well, since no sharp line of demarcation is anywhere evident.

The ordered complexity of living things certainly suggests intelligent design. Indeed, the entire universe gives eloquent testimony of being a product of mind and intelligence, as some scientists have maintained. Yet most of them believe that creative intelligence is the *last* thing to emerge, as the culmination of a long series of lucky accidents of evolution. Let us reverse this hypothesis and suppose instead that intelligence is primal, that the Cosmos is pervaded by intelligence. Not only does the idea make sense, but we come to realize that we have known it all the time. Such notions are by no means alien to us; they can be derived from our own experience, by analysis of our intimate modes of perception and thought. This is not some woolly hypothesis invented to comfort us. It is a matter of experience, as true as the beauty of a sunrise over the sea, though we may not all recognize our intimations or accept their implications. The aim of this book is to foster that recognition and to explain the implications; also to show that they can be supported by the writings of numerous scientists and philosophers.

These ideas have the further merit of being in line with the tenets of the great religions. The mystic does not need to be convinced by such arguments; he experiences for himself, if only momentarily, total immersion in the universal consciousness, the One Life. He is possessed by understanding deeper than words can convey. The scientist who allows intuition to guide his work is also under its sway, though he may not acknowledge it even to himself.

The first section of the book expounds these ideas and reviews in simple terms the old philosophical problem of what exactly we mean when we claim to know something. The relations between perception, thought, and intuition are considered, and the ways these are handled by the brain and its instrumental extension, the computer. The second section represents a fresh start at a logical beginning with the appearance of life on earth, while the third continues with genetics and evolution. The book seeks to demonstrate the untenability of some current ideas on biogenesis via random aggregation of molecules, and evolution via chance variations and mutations controlled only by natural selection. Those who have propounded such mechanistic hypotheses have usually expressed them only in general terms and have seldom pursued them in detail to their logical conclusions; when this is attempted, the hypotheses just do not stand up to unbiased analysis but can be demolished by *reductio ad absurdum* arguments. Some leading scientists realize that this is so, but most of them still cling to the materialistic theories they were originally taught, because they perceive no alternative.

It is here submitted that nothing less than the total inversion of orthodox ideas will serve. Innumerable mind-boggling difficulties are removed at a stroke if life and intelligence are accepted as the prime causes of the evolutionary process and not its product. The postulate of a primal cosmic intelligence provides a logical coherent framework for all we know about the creation of the universe and the emergence and evolution of biological life. Random chance is displaced by a nonphysical information matrix.

What has evolved is not intelligence itself but the means to express this intelligence through the brain and a body of flesh and blood. Primal intelligence became imprisoned in the mineral, stirred a little in the plant, unfolded in the animal, and became released in man. Intelligence reached its finest expression in self-aware man, with his capacity for creative thinking operating through his "new brain." But in man there is conflict between this new brain and the old or animal brain with its associated irrational instincts and fears. Thus handicapped, man has to face the awesome responsibility of planning his own future. For with the development of language and culture there came a dramatic change in the character and pace of evolution. Man now transcends his heredity and shapes his own destiny. No longer limited by slow genetic changes, civilized man now leaps ahead by what Julian Huxley calls psychosocial evolution.

Man has misused his powers in so many ways that he may soon face disaster on several fronts—overpopulation and undernutrition, exhaustion of natural resources, pollution of the environment, and threat of atomic war. If he heeds the writing on the wall there is just about time to avoid the impending doom. But there are some who prophesy that if he persists in ignoring the warnings, civilization may not survive long beyond the end of the century. With so much already achieved, it seems unthinkable that humanity should carelessly allow itself to become extinct. The final chapter attempts a synthesis of all the foregoing material, and concludes with an optimistic forecast of man's future.

Section One
INTELLIGENCE, BRAIN, AND COMPUTER

CHAPTER 1

"SEEING'S BELIEVING"

For normal everyday purposes we take for granted the objective reality of the world as we see it around us. "Seeing's believing," we say, or "I saw it with my own eyes," and it hardly occurs to us to question the accuracy of the picture our eyes provide. Yet there are many things we see that we should not believe, like rabbits appearing out of thin air at the touch of a magician's wand, and other optical illusions, recognized and unrecognized. On the other hand there are many things we believe but cannot see, especially if we are scientifically minded—atoms and electrons for example.

Our sense organs, especially those of sight and hearing, are incredibly complex, delicate, and sensitive. They serve us very well indeed, but nevertheless there are countless ways in which they let us down. Many of us are colorblind in varying degrees, and even more have some faults in the optical system of the eyes, partially correctable with spectacles. But even perfectly normal vision responds to only about one octave of the extensive electromagnetic spectrum, and sensitivity is far from uniform even within this small range. Some insects can see light of near ultraviolet wavelengths to which our eyes are insensitive. Their world must certainly look different from ours, even though there is only one actual world. Photographic emulsions are sensitive to these wavelengths and we can get a black and white rendering of what the insect sees. But if we try to use color film it just comes out excessively blue if there is a lot of ultraviolet light about, as in mountain scenes, and this is not a true rendering of "ultraviolet color." We cannot even imagine how colors would change if our eyes became ultraviolet-sensitive. Yet this would be only a slight extension of the visual spectrum. The world about us is "illuminated" by electromagnetic radiation covering many octaves to which we are totally insensitive. So how can we claim that we really see it as it is? All we know is what it looks like *to us*.

A very similar analysis could be made of hearing, though our ears do indeed respond over several octaves. But again, sensitivity varies over the range, and differs from one individual to another, particularly among the partly deaf. Young children and some animals can hear sounds higher in pitch than our normal range. Here, however, we can extrapolate in imagination and realize that such notes would be sensed as very shrill whistles. By adjusting the tone control on a Hi-Fi reproducer we can even get some impression of the overall effect that extended sensitivity would have on the sound of music: for most of us enjoyment would not be enhanced. However, that is incidental to the point that such high-pitched sounds are being made, by living creatures around us for example, but they are totally excluded from our own appreciation of the world.

Other senses, like those of taste and smell, are more difficult to analyze but the story is the same: our range of appreciation is so limited. In some animals the sense of smell is far keener than ours, while some insects are strongly attracted or repelled by substances we find almost odorless. Some birds and other migrating creatures may rely upon senses that we lack altogether.

Attention and Interpretation

But these quantitative limitations are still not the most serious of our sensory shortcomings. It has been truly said that we do not see what we are looking *at* so much as what we are looking *for*. In other words our sense organs are far from being passive scientific recording instruments. Two powerful factors are superimposed upon raw sense impressions; these are *attention* and *interpretation*.

The factor of attention is well illustrated by the experience most of us have had at crowded cocktail parties or similar events. We come into a meaningless babble of speech sounds, with everyone talking at once. Then we find a friend among the crowd and we hold a perfectly intelligible conversation with him. His voice may not be nearly as loud as that of a stranger shouting at our elbow, yet with little difficulty we can hear what we want to hear and ignore all the rest of the cacophony. What permits this remarkable selectivity? We usually turn the head into the best position, suggesting that both ears are involved, though the mechanism is not fully understood. But besides the technical competence of the receiving organs, there is needed a positive act of intention on our part. We have to *choose* to listen and only then do we make the conscious effort to utilize the resolving power of the aural apparatus. So we elect to pay attention, and this effort can be quite tiring if prolonged.

Dual Nature of Perception

This common experience brings home to us the dual nature of all sense perception. There is a *coming in,* of sound or light for example, and a *going out* to meet it, a deliberate switching-on of awareness: unless both occur no sense impression is registered in the consciousness. To pursue the analysis, it is better to consider the sense of sight because the mechanism of vision is rather well understood. But however closely we follow the chain of events there is always a hiatus; there is a highly significant gap of ignorance between electrical impulses in brain cells and a sensation of green, say, in our consciousness.

> The final event in the chain from the retina to the brain is a psychic experience. The transition from the excitations in the cortex to the subjective experience defies explanation. This psychic experience is a private phenomenon and in itself not subject to experimentation.[1]

(The word "psychic" is obviously used here in its literal sense of pertaining to the psyche, and does not imply any abnormal perception.) The sequence is familiar; white light of all wavelengths impinges on the grass of our lawn; some is absorbed, while light of certain wavelengths is selectively reflected into our eyes; it is focused by the lens of each eye onto the retina; there rapid photochemical changes occur in, for example, the visual purple, a retinal pigment whose chemistry is now fairly well known; the chemical reactions give rise in turn to electrical impulses which rush up the optic nerve to the brain. There the account gets a little vague; perhaps the electrical impulses are changed back into electrochemical reactions; anyhow we can suppose that the visual scene is reproduced in a large group of brain cells in some form that is certainly no longer light waves. There it remains, for a brief moment, before it is lost to the conscious mind and replaced by a fresh image, unless we choose to pay attention and scan the mental image. But what is the nature of this scanning by the consciousness? What makes an electrical impulse or a chemical change look green? This remains the unsolved mystery of vision. So what kind of right does all this give us to say that the grass *is* green just the way we see it? The mechanism of vision can, it is true, be probed a little from the other end. The electrical activity of the brain can be followed with an electroencephalograph which records a series of rhythms. It is easy to demonstrate that the rhythm changes abruptly when the subject pays attention either to visual stimuli or to a mental problem; but this extra knowledge by no means bridges the gap between the chemical and the psychological events, between chemical changes in brain cells and our awareness of the green lawn.

The mind's eye can still see pictures when the eyes are closed. These visions can be evoked in several ways: by recalling the memory of actual scenes; by deliberate imagination of "unreal" scenes; or by allowing the mind free rein when it will often create visual fantasies with no conscious prompting. How then do we distinguish what we are pleased to call "objective reality" from these latter which we describe as "merely subjective"? We assert that we can readily tell the difference, that impressions coming via the sense organs have a more vivid quality, and that only a person with a disordered mind could be confused. Yet a vivid dream can fool any of us at the moment of waking; the distinction is not so fundamental as we like to think. In the final analysis *all* immediate experience is subjective; it is *only* the subjective that we truly know as experience. The rest of what we know, or think we know, is *inferred* from those experiences.

This leads us to the second factor superimposed upon raw sense data, namely *interpretation*. We do not accept raw sense impressions just as they come into the brain: the mind first works them over, automatically for the most part. Messages from the separate sense organs are integrated, processed, and evaluated, all in a moment of time, so that the material is usually predigested before it is presented to the consciousness. This is so commonplace and automatic, so completely taken for granted, that the situation is hard to analyze. It is only the occasional failure that makes us aware of the process; only the totally new and unexpected observation for which there is no memory, no basis for comparison, is presented unanalyzed, with a sense of shock and warning, with an urgent demand for *conscious* judgment. We marvel overmuch at the speed and capabilities of electronic computers and not enough at our own: experience of the dim confusion following concussion of the brain is required to bring home to us what a superb instrument it is normally.

Some recent work by Dr. C.M.H. Pedlar at the Institute for Ophthalmology in London[2] shows that part of the processing takes place in the eye itself, before the visual images even reach the brain. As seen by the light microscope the nerve connections in the retina run from front to back, with few of the lateral or tangential connections that would be needed for a computer-like function. The electron microscope has now revealed an entirely different situation, with fine tangential connections estimated to number some 100,000 per sq. mm. This makes the retina look like a piece

of peripheral brain and justifies regarding it as an extension of the brain on the end of the optic nerve. It is now believed, accordingly, that the retina not only acts as an am-
plifier but also processes the information it receives before
passing it on to the brain. It is now seen that there are about
seventy-five structures connecting to the nerve fiber from
each cell. This function of the retina as a computer explains the relatively poor channel capacity on the output
side to the brain, i.e. the relatively small number of fibers in
the optic nerve. Economy is effected because information
not needed by the brain is suppressed by the retina and so
does not occupy transmission channels.

The Innocent Eye

If the retina functions as a computer, how is it programmed? The instructions cannot be permanent because
the nature of the discrimination needed will vary from one
occasion to another. Since we are not conscious of issuing
instructions, we must assume that this is a function of the
unconscious mind. This new knowledge makes a mockery
of the term "the innocent eye," the artist's eye that is supposed to take in a scene as a camera does, without applying
our habitual corrections. The image made by the lens on
the retina is not only turned the right way up, but is subjected to all sorts of adjustments and distortions before it is
ever offered to the brain for scrutiny. The artist may indeed
apply a kind of adjustment different from that used by the
nonartistic, but almost certainly some corrections will be
made. The state of consciousness needed to suspend the
automatic functions of the brain is the province of the
mystic rather than of the artist.

Which of us has not admired a landscape dominated by
glorious hills and sought to capture the memory with a
snapshot, only to find that in the photograph the hills appear insignificant? Primitive people can make little sense
of a photograph, because it is so different from what the eye
sees, or thinks it sees. Civilized people, on the contrary,
have subconsciously trained their eyes to see photographs
falsely as well, so that these seem to resemble the scene as

observed directly more closely than they really do, i.e. with prominent features enlarged, and emphasized also by enhanced contrast.

This additional information does not alter the fact that the point of consciousness still has to scan the image in the brain, and will do so selectively and in the light of memory. But the image it has available has already undergone a stage of predigestion, entirely unbeknown to our conscious mind.

For most purposes this instant interpretation is invaluable; but it is bought at a price. Most of us have practically lost the ability to "stand and stare," to see for example natural beauty as it *is,* entirely without evaluation, as a pure aesthetic experience, to look with "the innocent eye" as Sir Herbert Read puts it. Artists, musicians and such people retain some ability to do this, but for most of us, in the Western world at least, it is almost a lost art.

Two Components of Knowledge

It is important, then, to realize for ourselves, and fully to accept the idea, that "knowing" is a much more complex affair than we ordinarily appreciate. This attempt to analyze commonplace events may seem trivial and pointless. On the contrary, however, it is absolutely fundamental if we wish to assess the validity of what we "know," or believe we know. It is just such probing into matters we take for granted that can lead to fresh understanding. "Knowing" is made up of two components, totally different in quality but so closely integrated as almost to defy separate recognition. However, it is imperative to make this division, and moreover to make it in the right place, else the only result will be worse confusion.

In our example light waves travel from the sun via the lawn to the retinas of our eyes, where they are converted into electrochemical energy and thus conveyed to the brain. But the next step is the mystery; there is a sudden change from something we *know about* into something we *know* incontrovertibly, an experience in consciousness. Here then is the natural place to draw the dividing line: this is what distinguishes the two components of knowing. One is an inner experience, uniquely personal and *in itself* incommunicable. The other is our *description* and explanation of the experience, to ourselves and sometimes to others: it is everything that we know *about* the object seen, from past experience, hearsay, and science. These are emphatically not just two ways of describing the same thing. The first component is simply the *vision itself,* pure and unsullied by reason. It is not that the vision *cannot* be described, but just that the moment we start thinking about it, we have already moved over into the second component. No other man can see through my eyes. I can invite him to look for himself at the same object. If it is no longer available I can describe it so fully that he can conjure it up in his imagination, in his mind's eye. By comparing notes we can be sure that our visions are similar; but it is unlikely that they are strictly identical, and anyhow they cannot be compared directly.

It will be convenient to choose words for these two components of knowledge, and the choice of terms is important, because familiar words may have to be used in an unfamiliar way. If entirely new words were invented they would still have to be defined by known words, which in turn could be misunderstood. So the first will be called the *experiential component* of knowledge and the second the *rational component.* These two components are quite incommensurate, for they belong to different worlds of experience. But they are, of course, intimately related, and the relationship is one of mutual evocation. The personal experience (experiential component) recalls the rationalization; on another occasion the rational description evokes the experience in imagination. The two components are a bit like the song and the song-sheet: anyone who reads music can sing the song; hearing the song a musician can write down the tune. The song and its representation are totally distinct, yet they are components of one totality. But this analogy will confuse if it is pushed too far. (See also Northrop.[4])

Because sense inputs are processed by the brain (or even

by the retina on their way to the brain) before they are presented to the consciousness, it is not possible to draw the dividing line in this analysis as sharply as one could wish. It is inevitably a somewhat fuzzy band of demarcation, but it seems proper to include in the experiential component the registration of an event by the consciousness and, when appropriate, its recognition. Its naming, however, is part of the rational component. This seems logical because clearly memory is involved in the naming, as we realize when occasionally memory fails and we have to admit "the name escapes me." The lawn is registered as a slightly broken colored area, which we proceed to rationalize as a green grassy lawn.

So automatic has it become to exteriorize visual experiences that serious effort is required to realize that consciousness of the event really occurs in the mind. It may be easier to consider a different experience in which sight need play no part, namely hearing. If we listen to music, especially if it comes by radio or phonograph, there is no compulsion to refer it to the imagined orchestra or the reproducing machine. We can shut our eyes if we wish and recognize without difficulty that the experience of music is within the mind.

Reverting again to vision, our most highly developed sense, it is much more difficult to accept this simple fact that the final and crucial stage of seeing is also within the mind. From long practice we automatically and instantaneously analyze a scene as it presents itself. We make full use of our focusing system and binocular vision to give us information about distances and the sizes of objects: without any effort, after early childhood years, we see a scene in perspective. Then, automatically again, we exteriorize our mental image and project it onto the objects, pretending that is where the acts of vision occur. But all this is really vision *plus;* it is now hardly possible for us to appreciate for ourselves the nature of simple vision devoid of analysis and we must call upon the experiences of the blind to help us recapture it. Von Senden has surveyed case histories of people blind from birth who gained sight through an operation in

adult life, and encountered almost unbelievable difficulties in learning to understand what they saw; some indeed felt only relief when they went blind again. The first
reaction of one girl was utter confusion and disappoint-
ment. Here were new and bewildering sensations of light
and color, totally without discrimination or meaning initially. She had slowly to teach herself to apply the mental
element, the rational component that comes so naturally to
the normal-sighted, to learn to distinguish one patch of
color from another, to coordinate sight with touch, and
build up by persistent experimentation the sense of rel-
ative distance we normally acquire from infancy.

We may also learn from the blind how true it is that the
sense of perspective in a flat picture is a mental construct
and not a direct sense perception. It appears that people
blind from birth can, by patient instruction and experimentation, be taught to draw scenes in proper perspective.
At a certain stage of this training one after another of the
class attains an intuitive perception of the scene he has
drawn and becomes able to "see" it in the mind's eye, to
visualize it in full perspective, though his eyes have never
functioned. But much Asian and African art makes no use
of perspective, and most members of these groups (and also
illiterates in other countries) lack the ability to perceive perspective in Western drawings and in photographs.[3]

Direct and Indirect Knowledge

A final example may clarify exactly what is intended by
these terms "experiential component" and "rational component." We go into the garden and see a superb rose; we
observe and take delight in its exquisite form and color: we
touch it, noting with pleasure the cool smoothness of its
petals; we bend down to inhale its rich scent. There is an
uplifting of the heart, an expansion of consciousness, an
increased sense of kinship with Nature. This entire vivid
aesthetic experience, with so far not a word spoken, not a
thought   formulated,   constitutes   the   "experiential
component."

The description of the experience, such as we might give

to a friend afterward, is part of the "rational component." But even during the experience thoughts come flooding in, the word "rose," the name of the variety, recollections of previous roses on that bush—were they quite so large, so delicately shaded? One could write a little book about it, dealing with botany, breeding, cultivation, pruning, and so forth. *All* this could be comprised in the rational component of the event; but it still enters if we do no more than merely objectivize the experience as being caused by a lovely rose. Or we might turn to analyzing the sense channels through which the integrated experience came. But all this too comes within the rational component because it is something we know *about* from scientific reading, or from reflections on previous remembered events; it is not part of this direct inner experience. The experiential component includes nothing at all outside our immediate direct inner awareness. We may wonder how "true" is this component. But really this is a problem without meaning: of itself the experiential component of an event cannot be either true or false. It simply *is* for the living moment; it is our very life for that instant of time; if we argue afterwards, it is merely about our *memory* of it. Hence we may come to the following conclusion: the two components cannot be equated with one another; what is more, neither of them, nor even both together, can be equated with the object itself. Each way of knowing is an incomplete rendering of the object of attention, and this, if we stop to think about it, is a matter of common experience. For we can enlarge our knowledge of the one type by closer inspection, and of the other by reading or by scientific experimentation. But as noted, our channels of perception are incapable, even when integrated, of presenting the object in its totality to the mind's eye. Moreover the image is unique to the individual observer, being dependent upon the physiology of his optical systems and other sense channels, and his state of consciousness. Also, science expands, so we are never likely to know everything about it either. These should be humbling thoughts, but we do not reflect upon them often enough. Are we then doomed for all time to inhabit a kind of moonlit world? It will be suggested later that means can be developed to establish more intimate relationships.

Summary

Searching introspection reveals that we use the terms "subjective" and "objective" too loosely. In the last analysis, all knowledge of the world is subjective, but it is dual in character. The eyes and other sense organs convey their impressions to the brain for inspection by consciousness. This is immediate direct knowledge personal to the individual and in itself incommunicable, the experiential component of knowledge. Then the mind interprets these images at lightning speed, comparing them with past experiences, naming the objects seen and recalling all it knows about them; this is indirect inferred knowledge which is usually shared by others, the rational component of knowledge. The two components are incommensurable: both are needed to provide the fullest information that is available to us of the world around.

REFERENCES

[1]K.N. Ogle, *Science*, 1962, *135*, 763.
[2]C.M.H. Pedlar, reported in *New Scientist*, October 3, 1966.
[3]*Science Journal*, December 1969, *5A*, 48.
[4]F.S.C. Northrop, *The Meeting of East and West*, Macmillan, 1946.

CHAPTER 2

INTELLIGENCE AT LARGE

In the previous chapter attention has been drawn to the gap of ignorance between electrical or chemical changes in brain cells caused by sense impressions, and conscious awareness of an event. Most scientists ignore this hiatus in the train of events from sense organs to the conscious self, but it remains true that we simply do not understand how we perform that most familiar of operations, achieving rapport with our own brains. It is also important to realize that there is two-way traffic across this interface between the brain and the conscious self. By paying attention to brain patterns we acquire information about the world around us. But in addition we decide from time to time to do something about it, to initiate action. To this end a command is sent in some mysterious fashion across this interface to the brain, where it is instantly translated into a complex set of messages to muscles resulting in movement of the hand, as in writing, of the mouth, as in speaking, or of the whole body in physical activity. A little self-analysis will reveal that it is not true, as some psychologists claim, that all action emanates from the brain and its extensions, but neither is it necessary for the individual to determine every action consciously; the brain can attend automatically to the routine details of washing, shaving, and dressing each morning, but one has to make conscious choice of a tie. Again, to drive by car over a familiar route, one can instruct the brain to get on with it; it will cope largely unaided with bends, inclines and ordinary traffic situations, while one thinks or speaks of other things. But let an emergency arise and one must pay full attention to driving and initiate conscious action to avert an accident. In computer terms, the brain can be programmed for the routine operations, but a fresh program must be issued to deal with an unexpected situation.

Thus in familiar experience intelligence is associated with animal and human organisms, yet is quite distinct from them. We do not even understand how the gulf between them is bridged when intelligence acts on matter or uses the sense organs to gain information. Intelligence exists in its own domain, in a new dimension, to use an overworked phrase in a figurative rather than a strictly mathematical sense. It is not that intelligence operates in space with an extra dimension, but rather that it roams freely, untrammelled by either space or time. In its aspects of memory and imagination it appears to flit instantly from place to distant place, from the present to past or future, although of course thought does not actually travel to the scene imagined. We seem to live in an ocean of intelligence; our individual minds are pools within that ocean, somewhat insecurely partitioned off from the rest. Unplanned thought transference is far more common than is generally appreciated; we are constantly receptive to the unspoken thoughts of others, though it is true that we often fail when we attempt deliberate thought reading, because the conscious effort inhibits the knack.

These ideas about intelligence at large do not represent some abstruse philosophical hypothesis, but something readily deduced from everyday experience. If they are unfamiliar this is only because we do not pay close attention; we are so near to these matters that we accept them without question. Having ventured so far, it seems profitable to extend the analysis into somewhat more speculative fields. It has been said that a scientific hypothesis is useless if there is no means by which it can be disproved experimentally if it is wrong. In the exact sciences this criterion is acceptable, but in other fields where it is inapplicable man's thirst for understanding is too great for him to refrain from hypothesis. Religion would be deemed useless for the most part if this criterion were strictly upheld. In medicine, too, diagnosis of certain diseases can be proved with certainty only at autopsy; yet the hypothetical diagnosis can be exceedingly valuable if it leads to treatment that prolongs the patient's life. Similarly, at death we may be able to prove for ourselves whether our personal pool of intelligence survives. Meanwhile it can be intellectually satisfying to see if the hypothesis accords with, and reveals order within, the mass of circumstantial evidence that is available.

Intelligence Beyond the Brain

If human intelligence inhabits its own domain, associated in some ill-comprehended fashion with the brain and body but not of their nature, then what justification is there to follow the materialists in their assertion that it disappears with the death of the body? There seems to be enough evidence for survival without drawing upon the extensive but questionable testimony of spiritualism or reincarnation memories. Many people have "died" from drowning or heart failure and have been resuscitated by such means as the kiss of life or heart massage. They would have been pronounced dead by all previously accepted criteria, yet they have usually returned unchanged, with intact memories and all the individual behavior characteristics by which their families recognize them. It is true that resuscitation is completely successful only when no irreparable brain damage has occurred, confirming that the brain is certainly the essential instrument of our two-way commerce with the world. The question is whether it is possible to go along with the materialist who regards the brain as the seat and origin of *all* thought and action. As noted earlier, it does indeed appear that the brain can repeat thoughts and can direct action of an automatic character, unaided; other examples are the disorganized thinking in dreams and bodily movements in sleep. But most writers who have faced the problem agree that creative thinking and feelings of spiritual quality appertain to the intelligence. If this is not part of the body, then it must survive dissociation from the body at death and become reassociated on resuscitation.

The nature of memory will be considered in later chapters, but it is generally assumed by physiologists that all memories are inscribed somehow in brain cells, though it is then hard to explain why local brain damage does not eliminate specific groups of memories. Recent experiments with animals do suggest that learning simple tasks may be associated with chemical changes in brain tissue. However, memory is an essential aspect of intelligence; if personal intelligence survives death, then some memories at least must persist in noncorporeal form, even though they may have been recorded also in brain cells during life.

It thus appears that human experience compels belief in a domain of intelligence beyond the brain, which seemingly must also include the contributions of individuals no longer alive. It is presumably the seat of the "racial memory" that psychologists write about. Why then need it be supposed that this ocean of intelligence is limited to human contributions? It is a big jump, but a philosophically satisfying one, to suggest that intelligence is primal and cosmic, as the Buddhists affirm, for example. In human experience, cosmic intelligence is the source of the noble feelings, inspirations, and intuitions that arise unbidden within us from some superior realm; in biology it is the origin of the design and purpose that informs all living organisms. These themes will also be developed later. The mechanism of the interaction between cosmic intelligence and nature is beyond our ken; we have already noted that we do not even understand how our personal intelligence operates via the brain. It may be mentioned, however, that there is a little evidence for its direct action upon even inanimate matter, in the phenomenon of psychokinesis. For example, some people claim statistically significant effects of thought-power upon the proportion of heads that appear when tossing coins. Effects upon plants and animals are much more difficult to authenticate, but many green-fingered gardeners and gifted stock-breeders declare that both plants and animals respond better when cherished, and that the effect goes beyond that of routine attention to physical needs.

Many biologists agree that it is becoming increasingly difficult to account for all the complexities of evolution in the plant and animal kingdoms by chance variations and mutations perpetuated, in Darwinian terms, by the selection of the fittest. Some kind of guiding principle needs to be invoked, and it is physically impossible for such guidance to have been inherent in the cells of the original primitive forms. Much as orthodox biologists dislike any kind of vitalism, there is really no available repository for the program except the cosmic intelligence, or whatever other name one chooses for this necessarily noncorporeal information store. Any objection that it is not permissible to postulate some *deus ex machina* that interferes with the laws of nature is easily answered: this interaction is itself a law of nature, hitherto not clearly recognized as such. It may indeed be precisely that which constitutes the phenomenon of biological life, which distinguishes the living from the nonliving. These themes will be expanded in the third section of this book.

Summary

Sense impressions are recorded in the brain and scanned by the conscious self, which may initiate action by the reverse action upon the muscles via the brain. Despite the familiarity of these events, the nature of the link between brain and consciousness remains a mystery. Intelligence is distinct from the physical organism; it is associated with consciousness and exists free in its own domain. There is some evidence that it survives death and that a general ocean of intelligence exists. It is rational to suppose that intelligence is primal and cosmic, the original cause of evolution and not its product.

CHAPTER 3

CONSCIOUSNESS AND BRAIN

Two related problems have engaged the attention of scientists from time to time. One is ancient: the mind-brain duality and the related issue of whether man is a spiritual being, with the freedoms that implies, or a programmed automaton. The other is modern: the enormous increases in the competence of computers, which compel us to consider seriously the possibility that we may soon be able to make machines superior to ourselves. Gone are the days when a computer could be regarded as an improved ready reckoner, useful for doing arithmetic faster than its owner could. Now we have, for example, machines that can nearly always win a game of chess unless the human opponent is of international championship class.

Modern science and philosophy present an astonishingly wide spectrum of opinions on both topics. Human consciousness is a primary experience for most people and it is obvious that the brain is its instrument; others will admit of no such duality. Answers to the question "Can computers think?" range from "Of course they can" to "Don't be silly." (See Chapter 5) The former diversity, concerning mind and brain, can be illustrated by quotations from two papers in a special issue of *Science Journal*.[1] The first is from the introductory paper by Donald MacKay entitled "The Human Brain":

> Certainly the marvel of exquisite complexity now being revealed by the study of our brains ought to add a new dimension to our respect for humankind. The question that might be

raised, however, is whether in the process we may not find ourselves eliminating or "debunking" other dimensions that are even more precious to us. If the secrets of brain function were to yield to mechanistic analysis, would this not prove man to be "nothing but" a complex machine, and his traditionally recognized moral dimensions a mere illusion born of this complexity?

I do not think so. Indeed I believe that to argue in this way would be to commit a philosophical blunder, and to stand the facts of our human situation on their heads. For each of us, the first datum to which our thinking must do justice is our own conscious experience. Only through our conscious experience do we acquire the data that enables us to theorize about our brains. If any conflict arose between our theory of the brain and the reality of our conscious experience, it is our theory that would have to be modified to fit the facts, and not the other way around.

MacKay goes on to suggest that the notion of any such conflict is fallacious. Even if a completely mechanistic explanation of a human action could be given this would not be equivalent to a personal explanation in terms of motives, thoughts and choices.

To argue "it wasn't you who chose but your brain" would be as absurd as to claim that a computer's behavior wasn't determined by the equation it was solving but by the currents in its circuits. Each explanation in fact reveals a true and important aspect of the situation which is ignored by the other. Both mental and physical categories of explanation are needed in order to do justice to the mysterious unity we call a human person.

He argues further that a mechanistic brain story would also not eliminate freedom of choice, nor prove any sense of free will we possess to be an illusion.

All this seems to be brushed aside by J.Z. Young in his paper on "Neural Networks" in the same issue of *Science Journal*.[2]

Certainly man has achieved marvels of computation by his symbolism and "abstract thought." But how much there is still that he cannot do. For instance, it is beyond the range of most people to consider that there must be something wrong with a language system that insists that we are made of two separate entities called "a body" and "a mind." . . . Evidence of the confusion generated by the mind/body pseudo-problem suggests that with self-knowledge goes much self-confusion. We literally *cannot* look at ourselves objectively. Our brains are taught from childhood to operate in a certain way and can only partly learn later to do otherwise.

Young goes on to argue that it is better to start with examination of animal rather than human brains, as a first step toward understanding the behavior of human beings.

Rejection of Reductionism

Many other scientists have rejected this reductionist view, among them such well-known individuals as the authors of the three quotations that follow. The first is from Sir Charles Sherrington, the second by Sir John Eccles, the third by a recent past-President of the Royal Society, Sir Cyril Hinshelwood.

Mind knows itself and knows the world; chemistry and physics, explaining so much, cannot undertake to explain mind itself.[3]

Contrary to the physicalist creed, I believe that the prime reality of my experiencing self cannot with propriety be identified with brains, neurons, nerve impulses, or spatial temporal patterns of impulses . . . . I cannot believe that the gift of conscious experience has no further future, no possibility of another existence under some other intangible conditions.[4]

Great advances have been made in understanding the workings of the nervous system, and we have a rough idea how that most subtle and elaborate of all computers, the human brain, performs its functions. The conceptions of molecular codes and the storage of information which have arisen from work on reproduction have stimulated fascinating speculations about the mechanism of memory and even about the ancient mystery of dreams.

But what remains utterly incomprehensible is how and why the brain becomes the vehicle of consciousness . . . . Some philosophers have wanted to talk away the mind-matter problem as a mere verbal confusion. I suspect that at bottom they simply attach no importance to the scientific description of things and are therefore indifferent to any divorce between it and the language which describes the world of conscious experience. If so, they are of course entitled to remain indifferent; but men of science presumably do not.[5]

Almost everyone who thinks about it at all, takes for granted that he has a mind of his own of a nature different from the bodily brain, which it uses as an instrument. The notion is implicit in our language; it also follows from the tenets of the Christian religion, among others. Nevertheless for those who have accepted the contrary ideas of the behaviorists and other scientists, it is worth marshaling the arguments. Let it be said at the start, however, that this is not a matter that can be settled once for all by rigid scientific proof. There is plenty of evidence, but none of it is completely incontrovertible; so each must finally decide for himself whether or not he finds it convincing. At the same time it is fair to point out that some widely accepted scientific theories are no more firmly based, since they rely equally upon indirect evidence—a situation not always appreciated by the scientists themselves. Theories about the way in which evolution operates come into this category, for example, as will be seen from later chapters of this book.

Hypnotism

Somerville Roberts[6] has collected a mass of evidence, largely drawn from the realm of hypnotism, which leads reasonably to a tentative hypothesis of a "psychical element within the consciousness in control of all perceptual activities," which is distinct from the physical brain. Unfortunately he proceeds to irritate the scientific reader by building upon the hypothesis, with the help of somewhat outdated scientific ideas, as if it were proven and accepted fact. The skeptic who finds he can easily pick a few holes in the argument is liable to think he has demolished the whole case.

There is, on the contrary, much suggestive evidence to be drawn from the phenomena of hypnosis. The hypnotic trance resembles sleep in some ways, but differs in others. In both, there is clearly some interruption in the normal flow of communication which characterizes the waking state. The most reasonable explanation is that the conscious individual loosens his hold upon the brain at the bidding of the hypnotist, or voluntarily in sleep. But the electroencephalograph (EEG), which records the electric currents due to brain activity, reveals that the condition of the brain is quite different in the two states (see Chapter 4). In sleep it is quiescent most of the time, showing the characteristic "alpha rhythm" of closed eyes; in the trance state the EEG does not register sleep, but the more complex rhythms of waking activity (despite the closed eyes), because the brain is paying attention to the hypnotist's commands.

In the hypnotic state the normal association of the rational mind with the brain is suspended, leaving it open to the irrational subconscious mind. While it is free from the restraint normally exercised by the rational mind the brain can give full attention to the suggestions of the hypnotist, who takes temporary control and is able to impose his will on the subconscious mind. This accounts for the willingness of the hypnotized subject to believe or do things that are irrational and sometimes absurd. He carries out the orders of the hypnotist either immediately or after coming out of the trance, as directed. In the latter event, the subject may find himself impelled by his subconscious mind to perform actions that perplex him, though if challenged he will produce spurious justifications for them. Or he may have been told that he will see people or things that are not actually present, and will duly see them and refuse to accept proofs that he is wrong; if necessary his subconscious mind will invent detailed descriptions.

A logical explanation of this phenomenon is that on being released from the trance the subject's rational mind reintegrates with his brain, unaware of what has been happening in its absence, so that it accepts as its own whatever instructions have been impressed upon the subconscious, and accordingly feels obliged to justify them.

The hypnotized subject may be told to open his eyes but

that he will not be able to see because he is blind. He may then walk falteringly, colliding with obstacles as if he were really blind; yet brain rhythms recorded by the EEG machine are consistent with those of open seeing eyes. Presumably the visual image is present in the brain, but the hypnotist has imposed a block on its further transmission to the conscious self.

It is not suggested that the hypnotist enters into possession of the subject's brain in the fashion that is supposed by spiritualists to occur in a mediumistic trance; the hypnotist merely imposes his will by words of command. This is consistent with the fact that a phonograph record of the hypnotist's voice may be just as effective as his actual presence. It is even possible to hypnotize oneself, in order to impress upon the brain some instruction that would be resisted or ignored in full waking consciousness; for example, an attempt to cure a bad habit by suggestion is more effective when the brain is partially dissociated from the rational mind.

Treatment of Mental Illness

Another example may be taken from some forms of mental illness. These can be treated either with drugs or by means of psychotherapy. The drugs can operate only at the level of the brain cells, yet they are often effective in bringing the disordered behavior back toward normal. In psychotherapy the mind of the healer acts through the mind of the patient, presumably encouraging it to reorganize the disorientated brain cells and to reestablish the normal links with the brain. Either method can succeed while treatment continues: the difference is seen when treatment is stopped. In the drug-improved cases the deprived patient relapses in most instances to his original disordered condition. But if such a case is improved or cured by means of psychotherapy—that is, through the action of the mind of the healer on the mind of the patient—the cessation of treatment does not usually lead to a relapse but the patient remains in the improved mental condition he had reached when the treatment was stopped. These observations support the conclusion that the brain is the instrument of the mind.

Again, amnesia amounting to total loss of memory of a long period of his life can afflict a person whose brain is healthy and undamaged. This condition cannot be cured by drugs or brain surgery, but may respond to psychological treatment aimed at bringing emotionally toned incidents to the surface. Such cases provide good evidence that brain and mind are distinct, and that an ailing mind is not necessarily the result of a diseased or injured brain. It is observed further that we may say that mind cognizes brain, but not the reverse. The body, including the brain, belongs—along with external phenomenal objects like tables—to what is sometimes called the not-self, that which is cognized by the self. It would seem nonsensical to reverse the order of this duality and suggest that the table cognizes the observer. "Yet those who contend that brain is mind, virtually do this."

Further examples of human behavior that seem to compel acceptance of a consciousness independent of brain and body may be drawn from certain forms of sex abnormality and the characters of identical twins. It is well known that some individuals exist whose sex is more or less indeterminate. Some very rare members of this group are true hermaphrodites, having both ovaries and sperm-producing organs within their bodies. Others are pseudohermaphrodites having the internal organs of one sex, but externally appearing to be of the opposite sex, and these only learn of their true nature when the normal hormonic activity appropriate to their internal organs starts to function at adolescence. Homosexuals are definite males or females, but their hormonal imbalance causes them to be attracted more to members of their own sex than to the opposite. In transsexuals the psychological sex reversal is even more extreme. They think and feel emotionally like members of the opposite sex, even to preferring the clothing of that sex. By the time adulthood is reached, according to Dr. Harry Benjamin, "The crossover of emotion and thought may be so deeply ingrained that true transsexuals feel they belong to the opposite sex, and want to be and function as members of the opposite sex, not only to appear as such."[7] He says also: "Since the mind of the transsexual cannot be adjusted to the body, it is logical and justifiable to attempt the opposite, to adjust the body to the mind." In this situation the body and its hormone balance are normal, and there is nothing at the physical level that should prevent the individual from accepting his rightful sex. His persistent desire to behave as a member of the opposite sex as completely and fully as possible seems explicable only on the basis of a personality distinct from the physical body. The only hypothesis available to explain this phenomenon is that man's personality is something independent of his body, that the mind and brain are separate entities even though they usually work together.

Twins

Most twins derive from separate fertilized ova, so that they are genetically different. More rarely uniovular or identical twins are born, which derive from division of a single fertilized ovum so that their chromosomal constitutions are identical. Nevertheless, it is well known that such twins may differ considerably in temperament. The most logical explanation is that the personality of each is distinct from the physical body and is not solely determined by genetics and environment. Those who do not wish to believe this, suggest that the pair must have been subjected to different environmental influences which might suffice to account for the personality differences. Such an explanation cannot however be invoked in the case of Siamese twins, which are inescapably exposed to the same environment by their physical conjunction.

An interesting case of Siamese twins who lived to the age of 54 years concerns two sisters who were born joined at the base of the spine, and had separate limbs and internal organs except for the rectum. Although it was possible to separate them surgically, they had always expressed the wish to be allowed to stay together even after death. They were completely adapted to each other and actually preferred this way of living. The idea of separation seemed to them not only a physical but a mental amputation. The most interesting thing about them from the mental aspect was that their personalities were entirely different. Mary was easygoing and carefree, while Margaret was high-strung and always worried about health and financial matters. They lived an active life with a vaudeville song-and-dance act in many circuses and variety theatres, and at fairs in Europe and America. Later they opened a gift-shop, but in 1949 retired from work. Some years later, Margaret developed cancer of the stomach and died from this disease in January 1967 in the small American town of Holyoke, Massachusetts. Less than two minutes after her death, her sister Mary also died. In this case the identical chromosomal origin and a joint environment of the most intimate kind were unable to prevent two very different personalities from developing.

Until a few years ago such a case might have been considered conclusive evidence for a nonphysical individuality. It must now be admitted that the argument has been weakened, though by no means destroyed, by recent work on extrachromosomal inheritance (see Chapter 10). Several lines of research have suggested that inherited physical characteristics are not after all determined entirely by the chemistry of the chromosomes in the cell nucleus. However, like the genes themselves, these cytoplasmic factors exercise direct control upon physical characteristics only, not upon personality traits. As one heretical biochemist lately expressed it in a paper in *Nature,* these are determined by life itself (see also Chapters 13 and 14).

Zen Meditation

An interesting experiment which strongly suggests the possibility of mental activity dissociated from the brain was recently reported on television. A Japanese monk was wired to an electroencephalograph to record his brain rhythms, and he was then asked to undertake a Zen meditation. Almost at once the machine registered the alpha rhythm, characteristic of the resting inattentive brain (see Chapter

4). A deliberate interruption by noise broke the rhythm for a short period, signifying recall of the brain to attention. Repetitions of the noise disturbed the rhythm to the same extent every time, whereas with a normally relaxed subject a series of interruptions would have shown diminishing effects on the record as the subject came to expect and discount the interruptions. Afterward, the monk reported that his meditation had proceeded satisfactorily and he had been unaware of the noises, implying that his consciousness had been withdrawn completely from the brain while remaining active.

More detailed investigations have been reported by Wallace and Benson[8] on thirty-six American subjects trained in the technique of transcendental meditation developed by Maharishi Mahesh Yogi. Each subject acted as his or her own control. During meditation they all passed into what is called a wakeful hypometabolic state, most of the metabolic activities measured being depressed below normal waking levels. Specifically, both the rate of respiration and the volume respired were diminished; oxygen consumption and carbon dioxide exhaled were both some twenty per cent below normal. There was a slight increase in blood acidity, but the level of lactate in the blood fell markedly, being almost halved in some subjects. The heart rate also fell by about three beats per minute, but skin resistance rose up to fourfold. Another interesting finding was increased blood flow in the forearm, presumably due to dilation of blood vessels. It is highly significant that many of these changes are the exact opposite of those that occur in anxiety states; in particular high blood lactate and low skin resistance are characteristic concomitants of anxiety. Subjects wired up through scalp electrodes to an EEG machine showed regular intense slow alpha waves (nine to ten per second) as they went into meditation, especially strong in the front and central regions of the brain, with occasional theta wave activity.

The authors emphasize that this pattern of changes is unique and is not paralleled in more than a few particulars in any other state of consciousness. In sleep, for example, oxygen consumption does diminish, but only after several hours. The blood acidity and carbon dioxide level in the blood both rise but this is due to shallow respiration and decreased ventilation and not to changes in metabolism as in meditation. In sleep the brain shows high voltage slow waves at ten to twelve per second (spindle waves) plus weaker waves at various frequencies, quite different from the meditation pattern. In hypnosis there is no change in oxygen consumption, and other signs alter in a manner that depends entirely on the nature of the suggestions made by the hypnotist.

In meditation there is a complex general integrated group of responses related to a highly relaxed state. This work leaves no doubt that meditation is a real and unique state of consciousness that can easily be recognized by numerous objective physical signs.

Language Unique to Man

Possibly the most compelling evidence for a conscious entity superior to the brain comes, surprisingly, from some recent new thinking about language. It appears that our ability to talk is more remarkable than we have appreciated. Some birds can indeed be taught to talk, but they have no more comprehension of their words than a tape recorder. However, birds and animals do achieve limited intelligent communication, by sounds as well as signs, among themselves and sometimes with human beings. The most ambitious attempt to establish communication with an animal has been made by Dr. J.R. Gardner and his wife at the University of Nevada. A young female chimpanzee named Washoe is being taught American sign language, as used by the deaf in North America. In two years she has acquired a vocabulary of some 60 words and has learned to use them correctly. She will even sometimes make two or three signs in significant juxtaposition, such as "open-food-drink" for "open the refrigerator." But this is quite different from conversation as employed by even very young children. It is coming to be realized that syntax, the ability to join words into grammatical sentences, which is the essential element of human conversation, is something we are born with and do not have to learn, but which animals do not have and cannot learn. Professor Noam Chomsky is the leader of this revolution in linguistic thinking; he refers to the difficulty of establishing "psychic distance" from something so very familiar as language. The central problem is how we extract meaning from a sequence of words, and how we instantly distinguish a jumble from an orderly sentence, even a meaningless one. Chomsky's favorite examples are "John is easy to please" and "John is eager to please," two sentences with identical surface structures but different deep structures. We recognize immediately that John is the object of the first but the subject of the second. Conversely "Ann ate the apple" and "The apple was eaten by Ann" have different surface structures but the same meaning. Infants can pick up a vocabulary by listening, but not this inherent ability to see the deep structure, to follow the buried grammar. These ideas rehabilitate the "ghost in the machine," the mind independent of brain that many scientists have sought to deny. For even such simple examples are beyond the comprehension of computers or unaided brains; only human consciousness can understand the complexities of language.

This work does more than merely point to the linguistic deficiencies of animals. It helps to establish a qualitative distinction between the human and animal kingdoms at least as great as that between animal and vegetable, or vegetable and mineral, a break that is not generally recognized in evolutionary theory. Man is not after all just a superior kind of ape. This distinction is correlated with the great differences between human and animal brains. Not only is man's brain very large in relation to his size, but it includes the highly developed frontal lobes that animals do not have. The occasional human being born anencephalic, i.e. lacking these frontal lobes, lives like an animal; he is an imbecile with no self-consciousness or reasoning power. These frontal lobes may therefore be regarded as the organs of man's unique mind.

The human spirit seems to crave unity; for example, Einstein's consuming ambition was to formulate a unified field theory. Correspondingly, we are unhappy about dualities; but the mind-brain duality cannot validly be resolved just by denying one of its components, mind. In the everyday world this and other dualities must be accepted. Yet our intuitions of an ultimate unity are also valid, but only at levels of consciousness beyond the concrete mind, of which most of us have only occasional intimations (see Chapter 6).

Summary

The reductionist view that there is nothing beyond the brain has been rejected by many eminent scientists in favor of a mind-brain duality. Evidence for a nonphysical mind is drawn from the phenomena of hypnotism, treatment of mental illnesses, abnormal sex behavior, and Siamese twins. In Zen meditation and transcendental meditation the mind is in control of the brain and the rest of the body including some of its autonomic functions; this can be demonstrated by suitable monitoring techniques which show the body to be in a unique state of deep relaxation. Recent thinking about the way we learn and understand language also compels acceptance of a conscious entity in man superior to the brain.

REFERENCES

[1]D. MacKay, *Science Journal*, May 1967, *3*, 42.
[2]J.Z. Young, ibid., 52.
[3]C. Sherrington, *Man on His Nature*, Cambridge University Press, 2nd ed., 1951.
[4]J. Eccles, Eddington Memorial Lecture, 1963.
[5]C. Hinshelwood, Presidential Address to the British Association for the Advancement of Science, Cambridge, 1965.
[6]S. Roberts, *Does Man Have a Soul?* Zeus Press, London, 1968.
[7]H. Benjamin, *The Transsexual Phenomenon*, Julian Press, New York, 1966.
[8]R.K. Wallace and H. Benson, *The Scientific American*, 1972, *226*,85.

CHAPTER 4

HOW THE BRAIN WORKS

There is no possible doubt that the human brain is a superb instrument representing the highest achievement of the evolutionary process thus far. Both components of the closely integrated mind-brain complex are essential for effective operation and the overall efficiency can be limited by either. One is familiar with mentally lazy individuals who have potentially good minds but decline to stretch their brains to full capacity. There are others whose minds are unable to exhibit their full capabilities because of a defective or damaged brain. The very perfection of the instrument, and the observations that interference with the brain by surgery, electrical stimulation, or drugs can affect the expression of personality, have misled some scientists into supposing that the brain alone is a sufficient explanation of human behavior. But to offer a crude analogy, vision may be impaired by dark glasses, or ones containing unsuitable lenses; we are not thereby impelled to infer that vision resides in the spectacles. This chapter attempts to describe in simple terms some modern research on the brain, but it is necessarily more technical than previous chapters.

The Old and New Brain

When we come to consider how the brain functions, we meet at once a baffling problem: we really have not just one brain but two, which normally work together but are sometimes in conflict. There is first the old or primitive brain which is purely animal in its functions; it deals with the maintenance and preservation of the physical body, with its animal needs and urges and the emotions these arouse. Then secondly there is the much more recently evolved new or higher brain that is unique to man. It consists of the cerebral hemispheres of the human brain, much larger and more highly developed than in animals, and particularly the prefrontal lobes; it deals with intellectual activities of the self-conscious mind, both the concrete and perceptual thought pertaining to what is sometimes called the lower mind, and the abstract—including illumination and spiritual enlightenment—pertaining to the higher mind. These two organs, so tremendously different in function, are frequently lumped together as "the brain." This leads to constant confusion in general conversation and writing, even in some scientific books and articles. When we consider mind in relation to the brain it is the new brain we mean. MacLean has gone so far as to coin the term "schizophysiology" to emphasize the difference between the two parts of the brain, defining it as

> . . . a dichotomy in the function of the old and new cortex that might account for differences between emotional and mental behavior. While our intellectual functions are carried on in the newest and most highly developed part of the brain, our affective behavior continues to be dominated by a relatively crude and primitive system, by archaic structures in the brain whose fundamental pattern has undergone but little change in the whole course of evolution, from mouse to man.

In a paper read at the Fourteenth Nobel Symposium (Stockholm, 1969) Arthur Koestler quoted this passage and commented:

> The hypothesis that this form of schizophysiology is built into our species could go a long way to explain intraspecific warfare and the split between reason and emotion. The delusional streak in our history, the prevalence of passionately held irrational beliefs, would at last become comprehensible, could be expressed in physiological terms, and become ultimately accessible to physiological remedies.

Thus a modern scientist and a philosopher quoting him interpret St. Paul's eloquent lament:[1]

For the good that I would I do not; but the evil which I would not, that I do.

I find then a law, that, when I would do good, evil is present with me.

For I delight in the law of God after the inward man:

But I see another law in my members, warring against the law of my mind, and bringing me into captivity to the law of sin which is in my members.

It follows from the duality of our brains that although experiments with animals may have some bearing on those aspects of human behavior that are controlled by the old brain, they can have no relevance whatever to the more truly human activities of our new brain. In addition much of the relatively primitive research on the human brain is likewise concerned only with the old brain. Yet it is the working of the new brain, the seat of the human mind, that we so desperately need to understand better; survival of the human race itself may indeed depend upon it.

Pain, fear, hunger, fatigue, aggression, the mating instinct and so forth, are all needed for preservation of life and continuance of the race, but they are controlled primarily by the centers in the old brain; that is to say, they pertain to the animal-primitive brain complex and not to the mind and new brain. This does not mean that we have no effective control over such functions or that we need accept no responsibility if the misuse of any of them injures others. They can certainly be influenced by the mind, but the mind is not their originator.

Location of Brain Functions

Some of these functions can be assigned precise spatial locations in the primitive brain, which were mostly discovered by electrical stimulation experiments. An interesting example concerns the demonstration of a well-defined "aggression center" in human beings as well as in animals. A normally friendly cat when stimulated in the lateral hypothalamus by electrical impulses passing through wires implanted in the brain, would make a fierce attack upon a rat in its cage, but ignored the experimenter. But if stimulated through other leads also in the hypothalamus but nearer the midline of the brain, the cat would ignore the rat but attack the investigator instead.

Similarly a woman during the course of treatment involving exposure of the brain, was subjected to electrical stimulation. When this was applied to the amygdala in the temporal lobe she became abusive and aggressive toward her surgeon. When the current was turned off she reverted to her normal mild manner and apologized for her outburst; she described the experience as painless but unpleasant. In this patient hostile feelings and actions could be turned on or off by a switch in a frighteningly direct and immediate manner. Conversely, violent psychotics can be calmed down by electrical stimulation of other parts of the brain through permanently implanted electrodes. The patient, though unaware of the current, immediately relaxes and smiles and loses his aggressiveness. It is even feasible to provide the patient with a transistorized power pack through which he can himself switch off his hostility whenever it threatens to come on. It is well known that hostility can be aroused in other ways, though more slowly; for example, through oratory, martial music, and pictures; also through stress, frustration, and pain, and by some hormones and drugs. Alternatively hostility can be damped down by other drugs, such as Librium, that are not general tranquilizers and do not suppress cerebral activity, but act selectively on the aggression circuits in the brain.

The location of centers associated with such functions as muscular control, the five separate senses, coordination of movement, heartbeat, blood pressure, and numerous other vital activities, have been determined with almost pinpoint accuracy. Yet although areas controlling speech and writing have become well mapped out, these have dealt with muscular control only, and no center has been found that knows the meaning of words, or controls the formulation of ideas. Also, in the matter of memory, no special "box" equivalent to the computer's "memory store" has been identified; nor is memory to be found in a particular cell, synapse, or chemical molecule. When the brain is injured, even seriously, this does not cause a loss of *specific* memories; in fact none of the propensities of the human mind can so far be associated with any particular brain center. *In these respects the mind appears to stand alone exercising its supreme characteristic of intelligence, while the brain at the physical level simply provides the means of its expression.*

Memory Molecules

One of the most fascinating but frustrating areas of brain research is the study of memory, and in particular attempts to uncover the matrix upon which the memory trace is inscribed and the mechanism of its writing. It would be an understatement to say that there is a long way still to go, for many of the experimental results have received no adequate explanation, while others have been given two or more contradictory ones by different research teams. Most of this work has involved animals rather than men, including some lowly species such as flatworms, so the results have only a limited relationship with human memory. Readers who disapprove of experiments on animals may prefer to skip this section.*

Obviously one cannot teach a mouse to recite a poem; only simple locomotory or manual skills can be taught. Lower animals may, for example, be taught to find their way through some fairly simple maze. The method is to expose the creatures to the experimental conditions and let them wander about at random; after a period, those who happen to have reached the goal may be "rewarded," usually with food, or those who have not succeeded may be "punished," usually by an electric shock. Alternatively, the creatures may be exposed to a burst of sound or light, followed after a brief interval by an electric shock which they can avoid by moving swiftly to another part of the cage. After numerous repetitions they learn to traverse the maze correctly most times, or to take shock-avoiding action in re-

*Use of this material does not imply approval or disapproval of experimentation with animals. It is included for its valuable support of the book's thesis. Ed.

sponse to the warning sound or light. Higher animals may be taught to discriminate between shapes or colors, or to press a lever a certain number of times, or even to manipulate complex traps, again in order to obtain food as a reward, or to avoid a shock. Such learning is no more than the creation of conditioned reflexes and involves little if any reasoning; the animal does not know why it behaves as it does. It is difficult to suggest human equivalents, because we almost always learn consciously by actively imprinting the lesson on the memory, and not in this unself-conscious fashion. However, an infant learning to avoid fire after having been burned might be a fair example. Such reflexes involve only the "old brain," which we share with the animals, and not the more recently evolved parts associated with human intelligence and complex memories.

A good deal of research has gone into trying to locate the area of the brain corresponding with a particular lesson and defining the anatomical structures and physico-chemical processes involved in learning. It is well known that the brain is composed of specialized nerve cells called neurons; there are about ten thousand million of them in a human brain—a number equal to three times the present population of the world. Each neuron makes contact with thousands of others through specialized junction regions known as synapses. Nervous communication occurs in the form of electrical impulses that are said to "fire" a synapse and so establish communication between the interconnected neurons. J.Z. Young has gone so far as to postulate a "memory unit" somewhat analogous to an electronic computer unit and comprising a group of neurons linked by a complex circuit. Such a unit would represent only a first step, however, for it is generally recognized that memory must be inscribed in something more permanent than circulating electrical impulses. It is supposed that an electric charge "flips" a neuron into an excited state in which it becomes more reactive chemically; the memory trace must presumably persist in the form of chemical molecules of one kind or another. This idea has suggested in turn the exciting notion that learning might perhaps be transferable from one animal to another by brain extracts, and that these might be fractionated to determine the chemical nature of the "memory molecules."

Several research groups in America and others in England, India, and Sweden have worked with animals, mainly rodents, in attempts to determine the nature of the chemical molecules that are presumed to encode the memory traces corresponding to acquired learning. This work was inspired by the discovery that the genetic code, which can be regarded as the cellular memory of the species, is expressed by the order in which four nucleotides occur in the long chains of DNA (deoxyribonucleic acid) comprising the chromosomes of the cell nucleus (see Chapter 9). It is also known that the code is transcribed into nucleotide sequences in RNA (ribonucleic acid) and that this in turn specifies the sequence of amino acids that are built into peptide and protein molecules as they are synthesized in the cell. If it is permissible to argue by this analogy (and it may not be) then DNA, RNA, and protein are all possible candidates as "memory molecules." It is disconcerting to find that all of them have been assigned this role by one research team or another.

Three types of experimental approach have been used. First, it has been claimed that administration of certain drugs before the training sessions slows down or prevents learning; azaguanine and the antibiotic puromycin, which inhibit protein synthesis, are effective in this respect. However, these substances act in other ways besides inhibiting protein synthesis in the brain. Incidentally the converse effect has also been claimed, namely a drug that enhances RNA synthesis and also speeds up acquisition and the duration of memories in animals. It was also said to improve the memories of senile human patients with severe memory deficiencies. The second approach is to stimulate or train animals, then kill them and perform speedy chemical analyses of their brains compared with those of controls. Increased syntheses of RNA and of protein have been detected.

In the third type of experiment, brain extracts from

trained animals have been subjected to chemical separa-
tions and selected fractions injected into naive animals, resulting in these animals acquiring the appropriate
memory either without being trained at all or after only a
few training trials. Some of the results of such experiments
appear convincing but they have proved somewhat erratic;
they often fail when tried in other laboratories and sometimes even on repetition in the originating laboratory.
Moreover, as one group commented "our results do not indicate whether they involve the specific transfer of a
memory trace or the non-specific facilitation of conditioning." This second possibility recalls the "memory drug"
mentioned above. The most dramatic work is that of Ungar
and his colleagues at Houston, Texas.[2] Their experimental situation exploits the fact that a rat normally pre-
fers the dark; if placed in a lighted box it would run
through a short connecting passage into a dark box. But
each time it did so a door was slammed down and it received an electric shock; this was repeated until the animal
became more afraid of these experiences than of the light
and learned to stay in the lighted box. Ungar *et al.* claim
that the basic emotion of fear of the dark can be transferred
by a peptide isolated from the brains of trained rats, which
they call scotophobin. Moreover they claim to have fully
characterized and synthesized this molecule containing
fourteen amino acids, and that the synthetic and natural
products have identical biological activities. However,
both chemical and biological aspects of this work have been
severely criticed.[3,4] By and large it may be said that attempts
to reduce memory to biochemistry are not very convincing—a conclusion with which many scientists agree.

Nonphysical Memory Matrix

The animals learn their tasks rather slowly by the conditioning technique using rewards or punishments. By contrast Dr. John and his group at the New York Medical College found that cats could learn a trick very much more
quickly simply by watching other cats performing or
undergoing conditioning. Such observational learning is

probably the normal way of picking up knowledge, and these findings tend to discredit the usual conditioning method of training, as an unnatural process irrelevant to normal learning. Another possibility that has been ignored is telepathy, because most of the experimenters do not believe in it anyhow; it would in any event be difficult to exclude from the experimental set-up. There are innumerable examples of gregarious creatures, flocks of birds, for example, acting in concert as if they shared a group consciousness. It therefore does not seem too far-fetched to suggest that animals undergoing conditioning might convey what they learn telepathically to other animals in the same laboratory, especially when they are of the same species or even of one family. This seems particularly credible when fear is employed as a training device, as is often done. When an experimenter seeks to transfer learning via a brain extract, he will have a very clear idea of how he hopes the recipient animals will behave, and again it is not inconceivable that the "transfer" may be made telepathically from man to animal. Many people believe they have established telepathic rapport with their domestic pets. Again, it is well known among big game hunters and animal trainers that wild animals can pick up the fear or calmness of the human being concerned and act accordingly.

The conflicting results of all this work on the nature of memory might be reconciled by an explanation that does not seem to have been seriously considered, namely that the permanent master-trace of the lesson that has been learnt is inscribed in some nonphysical matrix, such as the mind, associated with the brain. Its recording in brain-cells for operational use could then be a secondary event, and moreover one that could be renewed if necessary. Transfers could then take place either at this nonphysical level, or perhaps at the physical level via a brain fraction. It is perhaps not too remarkable that some hormone-like substance may induce fear of the dark, or a tendency to turn left rather than right in a maze, or some similar reflex. It may be questioned whether such trivial learning should be dignified by the term "memory" at all, which in ordinary parlance designates the vastly more complicated human feats involving the new brain. But the scientific usage is wider, having been applied even to nonliving materials such as plastics, which can sometimes retain a "memory" of previous treatments and, for instance, revert to a former shape when heated.

Human Memory

One attempt to account for the nonspecific location of memory in the brain has been by analogy with optical holography. Invention of the laser, which emits coherent light, permits the recording of a scene not as a normal photograph but as a holograph produced by interference of light waves. This provides no meaningful image until it is illuminated in a special way by laser light, when the scene is reproduced three-dimensionally. The holograph has the peculiar property that the entire scene is recorded on every part of the film. Thus if a corner is cut off and removed none of the picture is lost; indeed the corner alone, if properly illuminated, will reproduce the whole picture though with impaired definition. If it is supposed that a particular memory is similarly recorded all over the brain, and not as a localized "picture," this could explain why even extensive brain damage does not destroy the memory. This might explain spatial memories, but temporal ones are more difficult to accommodate; for example a pianist can remember every note of a long concerto in its proper sequence. Professor Longuet-Higgins has suggested how this too might be accomplished in the brain by what he calls a holophone, analagous to a hologram. As a model for memory it is not entirely convincing, but the hypothesis affords an interesting illustration of how a new discovery can suggest a completely new way of looking at a problem, which would have been altogether inconceivable even a few years previously. Perhaps we need another totally new discovery to suggest the true nature of memory.

In the summer of 1970 *New Scientist* published an interesting sequence of short papers each from an exponent of a particular discipline used to study the brain.[5] It appears that despite a great deal of work we still do not know at all clearly how the brain operates. When workers in the more physical disciplines consider memory and its possible correlation with chemical molecules, they mean the most primitive aspects of memory, usually conditioned learning. This is a function of the old brain and they usually study animals rather than man. The physiologist, however, is obliged to consider more complex human feats of observation and recall that involve the new or truly human brain. This is a whole order of evolution beyond the primitive animal brain studied by his colleagues, whose findings have little if any application to human memory.

"Searching for memory traces is like looking for the difference between jazz and symphonic music by studying the humps on a gramophone record." "Science may never find the stuff of which memory is made; it is not composed of only material. It is also hidden in the process." "All experience is not stored in the brain. If people stored all the nonsense they have ever seen they could never retrieve anything." These three statements were made by scientists participating in a conference on the future of brain sciences, held in New York in May 1968. The last seems particularly significant. Despite the enormous storage capacity of the brain (see next chapter) it is suggested that the retrieval mechanism would get clogged up if burdened with all the trivia we have briefly recorded and swiftly forgotten. Yet the details of such observations are in fact not completely beyond recall, for under hypnosis or psychoanalysis long forgotten memories can be recovered. So, if they are not recorded in the brain, where do they come from? Again, one is forced to concede a nonphysical memory store. Where else indeed is the vast amount of material in the unconscious mind? It would hardly occur to the psychoanalyst that it might be stored in the physical brain. If he knew about them he would probably be amazed at the confident beliefs of his biochemical colleagues eagerly pursuing their project at the Institute next door, their conviction that memory is exclusively encoded in chemical molecules like the genetic code, and that it may be feasible to isolate this unique memory material from brain cells.

Throughout evolution function has preceded the organ through which it is to be exercised. The organ is developed in response to a need. So why should it be different with the brain? In other words, did not intelligence come first, able to function in its own realm, then gradually, during the aeons of evolutionary time, fashion and perfect a brain through which it could express itself in the physical world?

Brain Rhythms

Another interesting area of research on the brain concerns its electrical activity. An EEG machine (electroencephalograph) connected to electrodes attached externally to particular parts of the scalp records various electrical pulsations going on the whole time at rates of around four to forty per second. With a mentally active subject the trace of these brain waves is complex, with rhythms of numerous frequencies superimposed. However, when the subject closes his eyes and relaxes completely, the pattern changes to a simple one in which the oscillations are strong, slow, and steady. This is the well known alpha rhythm. It instantly breaks up into the less intense but more complex pattern if the subject is asked a question, starts thinking, or opens his eyes. Actually only about seventy per cent of individuals behave in this way; fifteen per cent show no alpha rhythm, and another fifteen per cent show alpha rhythm at all times. It is generally supposed to be due to electrical activity in the resting brain, though its high intensity is puzzling. Recently, however, Lippold has advanced arguments and experimental support in favor of his hypothesis that the alpha rhythm derives from oscillations of the eye muscles and not in the brain at all, which just rests when it is inactive. Whatever else these brain rhythms signify, they are undoubtedly related to levels of attention. Some subjects, while linked up to an EEG machine, have learned how to switch the alpha rhythm on or off at command by relaxing or concentrating. The reality of this "attention center" was brought home dramatically to the writer when he became subject to involuntary hypnagogic images during a short illness. Images appeared unbidden during periods of relaxation with the eyes closed, and became something of a nuisance. They could be switched off instantly by opening the eyes (but only when the room was light) or alternatively by paying attention to something, for example, by actively listening to background music, by thinking out a problem, or even by just readying the mind for thought. No EEG machine was available but there is little doubt that these actions would have switched off the alpha rhythm at the same moment as the pictures disappeared. These observations underline the point made in Chapter 1, namely that information gathered by the senses is not effectively received while one remains passive; it just "goes in one ear and out the other" like the background music. It will not register unless there is the deliberate intention to take note of what is coming in.

Some work by Dr. Grey Walter's team at the Burden Neurological Institute, Bristol, seems to have uncovered a deeper level of attention, described as expectancy, which is associated with a characteristic brain rhythm.[6] This discovery arose from studies on the brain's electrical response to external stimulation, as by an audible click or flashes of light. Such stimuli often cause a succession of strong waves during the next fraction of a second; they may have an intensity of twenty microvolts or so compared with only about one microvolt for the normal rhythm of the attentive brain. When light flashes are presented a second or two after the click, no connection having been suggested to the subject, then the total response is the same as that produced by the two stimuli separated in time. However, if the subject is told what will happen, and moreover is required to operate a switch immediately the lights appear, then the response is very different. The first signal then becomes a warning or conditioning signal and the pair of responses become firmly associated. After the normal response to the warning signal a negative electrical potential slowly builds up, reaching a peak of some twenty microvolts when the second signal is due to arrive; it then falls abruptly to the base line level when this signal comes, and the required response is made. This slow potential change has been called the Contingent Negative Variation (CNV) or the expectancy wave. It is not a phenomenon limited to artificial laboratory experiments. It is possible to wire up normally active individuals and have them transmit these brain signals via a miniature radio transmitter. Then this expectancy wave appears whenever some limb movement is required, as in catching a ball. The subjects are already alert and paying attention so this must represent a more intense degree of readiness which has been described as a "get ready" or "wait for it" state. It is easy enough to recognize from everyday experience that such a keyed up state of superalertness does exist, and it is interesting that it can be detected by objective scientific instruments. Moreover there is something more to it than science catching up with the obvious, for these EEG techniques already show some promise in the diagnosis of certain types of mental illness.

Biofeedback

Green et al.[7] have devised a simplified EEG machine which multiplies the frequencies of the brain waves by 200 to bring them into the audible range, so that subjects can be made aware of their own rhythms. The relatively rapid beta rhythms of normal brain activity are converted into something resembling the sound of a piccolo; the alpha and theta rhythms give tones resembling those of flute and oboe respectively, while the still slower delta rhythm associated with deep sleep or deep yogic meditation sounds like a bassoon. Thus these four principal brain rhythms produce between them sounds bearing some resemblance to a woodwind quartet when their frequencies are increased 200-fold by this instrument. Green et al. have found that in some subjects hypnagogic images and other evidences of contact with the unconscious mind are associated with a deeper level of relaxation or reverie in which the slower theta waves appear prominently. It seems possible that it is in this condition that some geniuses have received their inspirations and saints their revelations, so it may be a state of mind worth cultivating.

Other research groups besides that of Green *et al.* have used biofeedback in other interesting ways to enable subjects to assume control of bodily functions normally ordered by the involuntary autonomic nervous system, and not subject to conscious volition. For example, heart rate, blood pressure, or skin temperature can be monitored by suitable instruments and the readings can be displayed on meters which the subjects can see, or they can be converted into audible signals. For fear of inhibiting the subjects by explaining that they are being asked to assume control of involuntary functions, they are often not told what the meters indicate but are simply told to see if they can make the meter reading increase (or decrease). Most people manage to succeed after some practice, even though they do not know what they are doing or exactly how they are doing it. In this fashion numerous subjects have been able to raise or to lower blood pressure or heart rate, or to raise the temperature of the hands by as much as 25° F. by increasing blood flow.

For many years yogis have claimed the ability to perform these and other more dramatic feats of bodily control, but the Western world has remained skeptical. It is of great interest to have confirmation of these additional powers of the human consciousness over its physical vehicle and to know that, with the help of biofeedback, they can now be exercised by ordinary individuals without arduous yogic training. In some instances they have retained the knacks of exercising these controls even when the guidance of the meter is no longer available. Besides its scientific interest, such work has extreme practical value for some individuals. For example, severe migraine due to excessive pressure of blood in the brain was alleviated by encouraging a patient to discover how to divert the flow of blood into the arms instead. For other patients, ability to control the heart beat brought relief of cardiac conditions.

Dreaming

It is now possible to determine whether or not a sleeper is dreaming, without waking him. The most useful instrument is again the electroencephalograph. The stage of dreamless sleep is characterized by strong steady slow waves and, from their shape, is called spindle sleep; dreaming changes this pattern to one of weaker waves of variable frequency. This EEG indication can be supplemented by the electrooculogram (EOG) which records eye movement; during dream episodes eye movement is rapid, as if the subject were awake and watching or participating in some dramatic happening. This has given rise to the abbreviation REM (Rapid Eye Movement) sleep to signify the dream state. Third, the decreased muscle tone associated with dreaming can be checked with the electromyogram (EMG). If the subject is awakened when these indicators are positive, he will usually confirm that he was dreaming, but only rarely if awakened at other times. Contrary to the popular idea that a dream is compressed into the moment of waking, and to statements by some people that they seldom or never dream, we all dream for about a quarter of our sleeping hours. Moreover we positively need the dream periods for our mental well-being. If subjects are deprived of dreams by being wakened whenever they enter the REM state they become irritable and mentally distressed the following day even though they have been allowed their normal total period of sleep. This condition worsens if the experiment is continued for several nights. When finally left to sleep undisturbed, they tend to make up for lost dreams by an abnormally high proportion of REM sleep.

These remarkable observations are repeatable and established facts, but one is left wondering why dreaming, which usually seems a rather senseless occupation, should be so important. According to the Evans-Newman hypothesis, REM sleep is required for a form of information processing in the brain; it is suggested that long-term functional reorganization in the brain, i.e. adding new information to existing memory stores—a kind of brain programming—must be done with the help of REM sleep. To put it more simply, the brain needs undisturbed time on its own to sort out the day's experiences and file them away in orderly fashion, just as the bank clerk needs to work on after the bank closes. There is good evidence for a short-term memory covering recent events, which is lost if the brain suffers concussion, for example. So the nocturnal processing may consist at least in part of transferring this material to the long-term memory store. After all, the human brain is the most compact and versatile computer ever created, so it is not surprising that in order to maintain peak efficiency it needs time off nightly to reorganize its memory store.

Two American medical men, R. Greenberg and E.M. Dewan, working in Boston, Massachusetts, thought of a way of testing this hypothesis.[8] They reasoned that subjects with severe brain damage who are successfully regaining their mental powers should have a higher proportion of REM sleep than others who are not improving. Aphasia patients who have suffered severe cerebrovascular accident or trauma appear to be suitable subjects. Their improvement is studied over weeks or months; it is not due to return of function to damaged brain tissues, but to new learning or programming (i.e. it involves undamaged brain cells not previously used, or being reused for new purposes). Improvement in speech production or comprehension can easily be measured, and because this involves adding new information to the nervous system, higher levels of REM sleep should be needed. Fifteen patients were studied, six definitely improving, nine not. The percentage of REM sleep varied over rather wide limits, but the averages for the two groups did show highly significant differences on statistical analysis, with the former group taking the more REM sleep, as expected. Nevertheless in view of the small number of subjects this work clearly needs to be repeated before it can be regarded as conclusive.

We already knew that dreaming is essential for mental health and it now appears probable that it is specifically needed for information processing by the brain. This represents a significant advance in our understanding, but reflection compels the admission that it still leaves the fundamental question unanswered: Why should dreaming help the brain to do its work? Perhaps a modification of the hypothesis may be suggested, namely that dreaming *per se* is *not* essential in this respect but is an incidental accompaniment to the brain's introspection, though it may serve other purposes as well.

It seems necessary to postulate a loose fourfold subdivision of mental activities during sleep, the components being much less closely integrated than during waking hours. Most workers in this field tend to ignore at least one of the four. First, the body with the "old brain" is generally recognized to have a kind of dim individuality of its own; it turns itself over periodically while it sleeps, for example, to prevent stiffness or circulatory difficulties. Second, there is the new brain associated with the concrete mind and the memory stores, third, the unconscious mind and, fourth, the human consciousness and abstract mind temporarily dissociated from its physical body and free in its own realm. It can well be imagined that the brain uses the sleep period first, like the remainder of the body, to repair the cellular wear and tear of the day's activities; later the new brain turns in upon itself to do its filing free from interruptions. This leaves the body consciousness and the unconscious to their own devices, and this surely is when the dreaming starts, with the gates to the unconscious left unguarded by the censor.

To most people dreams seem inconsequential and not worth remembering; but the analytical psychologists profess to find them of great significance, although their interpretation is apt to differ from one school of psychology to another. According to Jung,[9] whose ideas seem the most convincing, the unconscious is the repository for all those elements of a total balanced character that the individual fails to express in his life. It therefore has a valuable regulatory and compensatory activity which it pursues mainly through dreams. Jung distinguishes three types of dreams: the first is sparked by events of the day which are reenacted with modifications appropriate to the supplementing or complementing activity of the unconscious; the second arises spontaneously in the unconscious and may create a conflict with the conscious situation of the moment, but with the two components evenly balanced; in the third type of dream the unconscious is dominant and may create dreams of special significance that may even, if remembered and understood properly, induce a change in the individual's way of life. Interpretation of dreams by a skilled analyst is held to be of particular value in the treatment of disturbed mental states. But all this dream activity presumably has no direct connection with the nightly activities the brain is believed to undertake.

Some people may object that one category of dreams has been omitted; they sometimes bring back on awakening vivid memories of what seemed to be actual experiences in another realm. If these are, as they believe, dreams in which the higher self participates, it would be expected that they would differ in quality from the normal inconsequential dream. Discussion revealed that the former, the so-called "astral experience," presents itself clearly as a whole continuous coherent event with a strong sense of personal participation; the other type of dream is comparatively vague, flits illogically from event to event, is recalled only piecemeal and with effort, and may present itself rather as something observed than as something performed. Presumably the human consciousness regularly encounters experiences in its own realm during sleep but only rarely are these impressed upon the brain and so recalled on wakening; when they are there is often an accompanying sensation of returning from far away.

Summary

The human brain is complex, with two distinct parts, namely the old or primitive brain inherited from the animals and the uniquely human new or higher brain comprising the cerebral hemispheres and prefrontal lobes, the organs of the human mind. This dichotomy may explain the sometime conflict between emotional and mental behavior. Experiments with animals necessarily concern only the animal brain, and have no relevance to truly human activities; much research on the human brain also involves only the old brain. Attempts to link learning in animals with biochemical changes in the brain have made little progress. Human memories are not located in any specific region of the brain and indeed there is much evidence for nonphysical memory storage. Brain activity can be monitored by its electrical rhythms, and various patterns denote thinking, alertness, resting, meditation, sleep, and dreaming. Brain rhythms, and also numerous physiological functions such as heart beat, blood pressure, skin temperature, and so on can be made to operate visual or audible signals. When these are displayed to subjects, they can learn with the help of this biofeedback to bring under voluntary command functions normally controlled by the autonomic nervous system. During sleep, a loose fourfold subdivision of mental activities seems necessary to explain various kinds of dreams and the brain reprogramming that appears to occur.

REFERENCES

[1]St. Paul, Rom. 7:19, 21-23.
[2]G. Ungar, D.M. Desiderio and W. Parr, *Nature, 1972: 238,* 198; 209.
[3]W.W. Stewart, ibid, 202.
[4]Graham Chedd, *New Scientist,* Aug. 3, 1972, 240; also 226.
[5]Anon, *New Scientist,* June 25, 1970.
[6]S. Barondes, *New Scientist,* Feb. 6, 1969:278.
[7]E.E. Green, A.M. Green, and E.D. Walker, *Fields Within Fields . . . Within Fields,* 1972, *5,* 131.
[8]R. Greenberg and E.M. Dewan, *Nature,* 1969, *233,* 183.
[9]Jolandi Jacobi, *The Psychology of C.G. Jung,* Routledge and Kegan Paul, London, 7th ed., 1968.

CHAPTER 5

DO COMPUTERS THINK?

Can computers think? This is a philosophical problem, which, as so often happens, can be reduced to semantics: it all depends what one means by thinking. Except when it is merely repetitive, human thinking is purposeful, and is almost if not quite inseparable from emotion. It is driven either from "below" by desire or emotion, or from "above" by inspiration. Pure thought is perhaps impossible for us; abstract mathematical thinking comes closest, but even here one does not tackle a problem without desiring the answer, and anticipating the aesthetic satisfaction of a solution. Men compute because they *want* to do so. We have drives, needs, desires that urge us to make calculations, for fun or for gain. In antithesis, a computer does what it is told to do; it is capable of nothing but cold mechanical "thinking," being totally without self-generated drive, inspiration, purpose, or emotion. To be useful a computer must indeed be programmed for a purpose, but this originates with the user and not with the machine; some talking computers can even be made to simulate emotion, but this derives from the programmer's imagination and has to be pre-recorded on magnetic tape.

The answer given by W.H. Thorpe[1] to the question in this chapter's title (already cited in part in Chapter 3) is "Don't be silly . . . computers manipulate not ideas but tokens for ideas—as presumably do brains." It is we who think, not our unaided brains, and moreover thinking is our very life. The human consciousness inhabits a realm in which ideas and related emotions are paramount. The realities of our realm are immediate percepts arriving via the senses but interpreted en route by previous experience, our ideas and feelings about them, and the memories and reflections they stimulate (see Chapter 1). This is a far remove from the soulless electronics of a computer.

Chapter 3 opened with two problems, the mind-brain duality, and implications of the possibility that computers may eventually be made that are superior to ourselves. It turns out that these two problems are related in the sense that one's attitude toward the first determines that toward the second. Thus for a reductionist, believing that the brain is the acme of human development and that its workings will in due course be determined along mechanistic lines, unquestionably computers do think. Moreover one must humbly acknowledge that in some respects they do this better than we do. Already they are superior to human brains in speed and accuracy, though much more limited in range; a whole battery of present-day computers could not encompass the diversity of an educated human brain. But the reductionist is inclined to believe that it is only a matter of time and further advances in microminiaturization of electronic devices before superhuman computers and robots compete with man for supremacy. This approach seems to leave no place for aesthetics, moral and spiritual values, heroism, altruism, and so forth.

If on the other hand one recognizes self-consciousness as the primal experience to which all others (short of cosmic consciousness) are subordinate, then one can laugh with Thorpe at the notion of computers thinking for themselves. The senses, brain, and muscles are agents of consciousness; just as tools can be regarded as extensions of muscular powers, and scientific instruments such as microscopes, telescopes, and radio as extensions of the sense organs, so are computers extensions of the brain. These things have no autonomy and are not themselves to be feared except when they accidentally get out of control. What is to be feared from their rapidly expanding capabilities is their willful misuse *by human beings* in positions of power.

Thinking Powers of Brain and Computer

The astonishing sophistication of modern computers can be accepted as a tribute to man's inventiveness. It is nevertheless interesting to note that some of their capabilities do lie in fields that used to be considered prerogatives of the human mind. Scientists who believe that computers may eventually beat us at the thinking game base their prophecies on the analogies between the operations of brains and computers. But Einstein has warned that in science, "analogies have been a source, not only of the most fruitful theories, but also of the most misleading fallacies." Computers and brains operate in different ways and excel in different areas. Moreover, cross-fertilization has occurred between researches in the two fields; computer circuitry has given some clues to the way the brain works, while, conversely, our growing but still far from complete understanding of brain function has provided ideas that may be exploited in computer design.

A fascinating comparison has been provided by N.S. Sutherland.[2] Speed is the computer's main asset. Indeed, it has few others except that it is more accurate and does not get tired. The computer does score, however, in a minor way by being able to delete memories, to forget deliberately; the brain cannot do this and so we become lumbered with bad habits, unwanted associations, and other things we should be glad to forget. The digital computer can accept and store information at a rate exceeding a million bits per second; the brain can process information from the sense organs at a similar or even greater rate, but its storage rate is quite slow, namely about one bit per second in the long term memory, although the evanescent short term memory is faster. The computer can transfer out information at a rate already exceeding 6000 bits per second, whereas the brain can handle only around 20 bits per second, as in fast typing, for example. The computer's elements are reset in one ten-millionth of a second, compared with one hundredth of a second for the brain. On the other hand the brain scores with its vast array of interconnections that enable it to process many lines of information simultaneously in parallel, whereas the computer with few interconnections is mainly restricted to serial processing. This clumsy mode is rendered acceptable only by its enormous speed; putting it the other way round, the brain does not need great speed because it can tackle millions of operations at once. By time-sharing, modern computers do give the illusion that they also can perform several unrelated tasks simultaneously. In fact, these are done successively, switching from one to another in sequence, but taking such brief moments that for practical purposes the effect is of truly simultaneous operation.

The storage capacity of the human brain, namely a theoretical maximum of a thousand million bits in a lifetime, is about thirty times greater than that of any existing computer, though there can be few men who fill their memory store to capacity, and computers are improving constantly. The brain's memory store is more readily accessible through extensive cross-referencing and "associative memory," a process that cannot as yet be matched by computers. However, Dr. Ian Aleksander of the University of Kent has already designed a model computer that can learn as the brain does, containing thousands of microcircuits that function like neurons. Again, the computer must be fed on predigested information whereas the brain has of necessity to filter the mass of raw data from the sense organs, to extract meaning therefrom, and does so very efficiently. Machines with sense organs that can recognize objects, printed and even written letters, are being developed, but are not yet highly advanced; moreover these capabilities consume much of their total capacity.

Even the best computers have strictly limited programs, and can only tackle a narrow range of problems; if only one component fails, the output is usually reduced to nonsense. The brain on the contrary, is enormously versatile, and even extensive injury rarely produces nonsense, or at any rate not permanently; after a period of readjustment, remaining components can take over the functions of those lost.

Creative Thinking by Computers

In view of these many disabilities of computers, the claim may seem surprising at first sight that they can develop independence and originality of thought and even exhibit creative thinking of an uncannily human caliber. Naturally a computer must always provide new knowledge to have any utility, for if one already knew the answer to a problem there would be no point in putting it up for processing. Earlier computers were given purely mathematical problems, complex but with unique right answers, so there was no surprise; the user would inevitably have reached the same result unaided if he made no errors in the hours or days of calculations involved. But this is no longer the ultimate; modern computers can be programmed to study alternatives and come up with a considered choice. For example, an architect might have a bridge to design, and he could feed into the computer all the required information about dimensions, strength, load-bearing capacity and so forth, along with costs of alternative building materials and methods and labor, and ask the computer to specify the cheapest solution. He could also perfectly well introduce aesthetic considerations, such as that a bridge with five or seven spans would look better than one with a different number and much better than one with an even number of spans, and that beauty could override cost to some degree. It is true he would have to weight and quantize these considerations precisely; but such weighting is also involved, even if only subconsciously, in any human choice. The machine could be asked to provide specifications for the better alternatives for the architect's scrutiny and decision. But in the ultimate it could be asked to make the final choice by itself, even if this involved arbitrary decisions between equally acceptable modes of construction. There are even computers available that would sketch out the chosen design besides printing out a detailed specification.

This capability to make a reasoned choice is fundamental to game-playing computers; these must naturally be taught the rules and basic strategies of play. With the earliest, playing noughts and crosses, it was possible to program for all possible situations, so that the machine could invariably win or draw. With the more complex games like draughts (checkers) and especially with chess, this is no longer possible and a good player can get the computer into situations against which it has no adequate defense. These machines can, however, be programmed to remember and learn from their mistakes so that their standard of play improves with practice, just like that of a human player. Here the element of surprise does enter, for these machines often develop strategies quite unforeseen by their creators.

Computers have recently been designed that can hold some sort of conversation with their users by typewriter. Some, for instance, can help doctors with medical diagnoses of patients. Signs, symptoms, and test results are fed in, and the machine can respond with several likely diagnoses and the mathematical probability of each being correct. It can also suggest the most critical further tests that could clinch the diagnosis. This can save time, money, and discomfort for the patient by eliminating tests regarded as routine but which nevertheless are superfluous. At present such machines cover only a limited range of diseases and are not really very helpful. However, their limitations do not lie in the electronics but in the associated human skills of the programmer. The machine capability is there, awaiting more imaginative exploitation.

Man and Computer

The computer does not displace the user; it augments him. The two working together can become a powerful team. As G.A. Miller puts it:

> As our understanding increases, I think we will be better able to optimise the man-machine team. Mechanical intelligence will not ultimately replace human intelligence, but rather, by complementing our human intelligence, will supplement and amplify it. We will learn to supply by mechanical organs those functions that natural evolution has failed to provide . . . .
> The gap between men and machines has narrowed—not by degrading man, let me repeat, but by enriching our conception of

a machine . . . . Always distrust the man who tells you that human beings are "nothing but" something else, for he is deliberately concealing from you the abstraction on which his claim is based. Human beings are nothing but human beings.[3]

Some of the conclusions reached by computers would, if they had arisen in human minds, be regarded as examples of creative thinking or even as intuitive flashes. Fortunately there is no need either to credit the computer with the suprarational faculty of intuition, or to discredit it in the human mind. The fact is that any intuitively-reached conclusion *concerning material things* could have been reached by straightforward reasoning; indeed it is always necessary to test such an intuition by seeking out and following through the appropriate sequence of logical steps. To reach its goal the computer must laboriously test and discard all unfruitful steps and finally arrive at the right answer; but its great speed still enables it to do so with an air of magical rapidity that mimics the workings of intuition.

It must be emphasized that this conclusion applies only to strictly practical matters and not to intuitions concerning scientific hypotheses or to artistic or religious inspiration. As the next chapter will show, these all contain elements beyond what is explicit in the facts of the situation.

Several contributors to the special issue of *Science Journal* for October 1968 offer somewhat fanciful forecasts of what future computers may be able to do. Sutherland, for example, suggests that we may before too long be able to design machines that are our intellectual superiors in general and not merely in isolated special fields. He argues further, though with dubious validity, that such a machine must, *a fortiori* be able to design one in turn more intelligent than itself. He goes on to discuss with what goals we ought to endow these superbrains and recommends intellectual curiosity as paramount.

> In 50 years time we may have ceased to argue about racial problems—we shall be too busy arguing about whether computers should be entitled to a vote.

In his introduction, appropriately entitled "Machines are more than they seem," Marvin Minsky writes:

The advance in the behavior of machines, over the past hundred years, was like a billion years of biology . . . . Do not be bullied by authoritative pronouncements about what machines will never do. Such statements are based upon pride, not fact. There has emerged no hint, in any scientific theory of machines, of limitations not shared by man . . . . Today, machines solve problems mainly according to the principles we build into them. Before very long, we may learn how to set them to work upon the very special problem of improving our own capacity to solve problems. Once a certain threshold is passed, this could lead to a spiral of acceleration and it may be hard to perfect a reliable "governor" to restrain it.

Indeed, perhaps we *ought* to hand over control to the computers, as Donald Gould suggests in an outburst of dark humor,[4] for we have made a sorry mess of running the world's affairs. Within the lifetime of our children we are threatened with catastrophic overpopulation and famine; exhaustion of mineral resources; life-destroying pollution of earth, water, and air; and enough atomic weapons to exterminate the human race. Yet we cannot bring ourselves to take effective action to avert these hazards. So let us replace our human rulers by computers. "Having no emotions they will be brave enough to face the truth."

A somewhat different angle on the problem has recently been ventilated in the pages of *New Scientist* in an article by D.F. Lawden entitled "Are Robots Conscious?" and ensuing correspondence.[5] The problem was not solved, and this is not surprising because the consciousness of robots seems to be a pseudo-problem. It vanishes as soon as one recognizes *degrees* of consciousness, the qualities of which can range from the scarcely credible dim awareness of a rock through animal alertness to human self-consciousness. An animal is subjectively immersed in consciousness, but to an educated man it is an objective phenomenon for wonder and analysis. The same author[6] had earlier argued cogently that since consciousness is for us an undeniable experience, and no really sharp dividing line apart from human *self*-consciousness can be discerned as one descends through increasingly primitive organisms to minerals, then consciousness of a sort must be accorded throughout.

If this is conceded, then the materials from which a computer or an engine are constructed already enjoy a modicum of consciousness. When either machine is completed and exhibits coordinated action in its functioning, it is not difficult to accord it a greater measure of consciousness; but surely its entirely automatic and predictable responses to stimuli put it hardly above the plant level. So have we anything to fear from things with a plant-like consciousness? Well, certainly plants can be powerful enemies, as when weeds choke our farms and waterways. But the analogy is imperfect; though machines, like plants, know neither morality nor mercy, the machines are entirely of our own creation, and we have the power and the duty to keep them firmly under control.

Most of these scientists write as though intellectual prowess leading to greater knowledge and technological progress is all that really matters, and for them perhaps this is so. But others have different attitudes toward human values, and fortunately for them, there remain realms in which the computer is entirely powerless and the human being is without even a potential rival. Aesthetic, artistic, religious, and moral values, and indeed any judgments that cannot be quantized are totally beyond any computer's competence. It is true that such values are individual rather than absolute, even though there may be a consensus of opinion, but to say this is not to underrate their importance to the human spirit; indeed, many people rate them far above any material values that come within the computer's ambit. The spiritual life seems forever beyond mechanization.

Summary

The digital computer is capable only of an on-off, yes-no, response, or in numbers, 0 and 1 only, dictating the use of binary numeration. This clumsy mode is acceptable only because of the computer's extremely high speed of operation and accuracy. Though it must perform multiplication or division by stepwise addition or subtraction it can still calculate much faster than the human brain. By contrast the brain, though relatively slow, is much more subtle in its operations, being able to process many lines of information simultaneously; also its storage capacity is enormous, and it has far better access to its memory stores through associative memory and cross-referencing than has the computer.

Modern computers can be programmed to perform creative thinking as in playing chess, for example, but there is no fear of humanity being made redundant by computers of ever-increasing power. Behind every computer stands a man: he is augmented, not displaced, by the machine. Moreover the computer is totally unable to make aesthetic, artistic, or moral judgments: the spiritual life can never be mechanized.

REFERENCES

[1]W.H. Thorpe, *Science, Man and Morals*, Cox and Wyman, London, 1965.
[2]N.S. Sutherland, *Science Journal*, Oct. 1968, *4*, 44.
[3]G.A. Miller, *Advancement of Science*, 1965, 417.
[4]Donald Gould, *New Scientist*, Aug. 6, 1970, 298.
[5]D.F. Lawden, *New Scientist*, Sept. 4, 1969, 476.
[6]D.F. Lawden, *Nature*, 1964, *202*, 412.

CHAPTER 6

BEYOND THE MIND

Chapter 1 describes how we gain knowledge of the world around us by direct observation via the sense organs, and the interpretation of these impressions by the mind in the light of previous experiences and preconceptions. But man is not content just to observe the world of nature: he is curious about it; he wants to know the how and why of things. Earlier civilizations mostly let imagination take over where observation ended. Their craftsmanship and technology were prompted by household and communal needs and by chance observations, such as the way minerals behaved in fires. Later, observations were catalogued in orderly fashion, marking the beginnings of botany and the other natural sciences. Recent centuries have seen a largely new development, namely the realization that man can find out for himself, can ask questions of nature by way of trials and experiments and so learn to understand her ways. This has led to the explosive growth of modern experimental science. The senses have been supplemented by scientific instruments to magnify, probe, and analyze with ever greater power and precision. Mental powers too have strengthened through practice and discussion, and understanding has deepened with the refining of philosophy. The practical outcome was the industrial revolution and our present advanced technology.

Induction and Deduction

Reasoning is supposed to relate to its practical basis in

two ways which proceed in opposite directions, namely by induction and by deduction. Inductive reasoning goes from the particular to the general, considering a collection of related facts and deriving a general conclusion that unites them within some coordinated scheme. Deduction starts from a general principle and derives therefrom particular events that should occur in specified circumstances if the principle is true. Such predictions can serve to allow or disprove a theory. For a century or more it has been generally accepted that these are the only ways in which science works. In other fields of human endeavor it has been quietly recognized that understanding can come in other ways than by stepwise logical reasoning, whether inductive or deductive. Ordinary people have their intuitions, when understanding of some problem comes to them in a flash without conscious mental effort. The gifted musician does not reason out his compositions. His melodies and the realization of how they can be developed and varied appear in his mind suddenly without prior rational thought. True, the details of the composition and its orchestration must be worked out and set down by normal laborious means, but the fundamental sounds are a gift from beyond the reasoning mind. The artist too, unless he is content with strictly representational art, acknowledges inner visions from time to time, which he strives to convey in his paintings, sculptures, or architectural designs. Many other people have such aesthetic ecstacies, often triggered by beauty of Nature or art, whether or not they have the ability to portray them in poetry, prose, or art of any kind. For thousands of years religious mystics have "spoken with God," entered Nirvana" or "attained cosmic consciousness." Evidently this mystical experience is more intense, more overwhelming, than a specific intuition or artistic inspiration. Mystics have recognized it as a state beyond normal consciousness in which separate identity is temporarily relinquished, and they are absorbed into union with the whole of creation. They become one with a universal wisdom so that for the moment they have full realization of many deep mysteries.

"Peak experience" is a useful general term for illumination at any level which is free from implications about mechanisms.

Naturally scientists are not exempt from the play of intuition. Some of the greatest have acknowledged their debts by admitting how theories that have changed the face of science appeared to them in a flash. One might expect that scientists would have turned their scientific attention to this phenomenon and would have provided clear explanations for the working of the intuitive process. In fact their attempts have been few and disappointing; possibly they are not introspective enough to analyze their own thinking, but most of them seem rather scared of the whole idea and unwilling to admit the operation of intuition even to themselves, as if ashamed to admit that their problems were solved by "cheating" instead of by honest logic! Certainly it is a recognized practice to write up research for publication as if the conclusions had been reached by strict application of inductive reasoning.

Sir Peter Medawar, a Nobel laureate, is one who does accept the function of intuition, and possibly the clearest analysis of the situation is that made in his Jayne Lectures for 1968.[1] Medawar points out that for a century or more it has been generally accepted that scientific hypotheses arise by Baconian inductive reasoning, whereas, he proclaims boldly, they can't and don't. Induction has its uses but is simply not capable of adding that essential comprehension which turns a collection of observations into a meaningful ordered synthesis. Having hit upon this synthesis *by other means,* the scientist does not usually admit it, but feels obliged, when he writes up his work, to act out the respectable pretense that he has reached it inductively. Inductivism has many shortcomings as a research tool. Its first injunction is to collect facts, to make observations; but a geologist gains nothing by going into a gravel pit to count pebbles and note their colors. It is essential to select, from the entire natural world, those observations likely to be fruitful and to design critical experiments instead of random trials. The inductive method provides no clues to guide the selections of either observations or experiments. Moreover,

> Inductivism gives no adequate account of scientific fallibility, fails altogether to explain how it comes about that the very same process of thought which leads us towards the truth leads us so very much more often into error, and that nearly all scientific research leads nowhere.

The scientific method is not really as powerful as it is often made out to be.

Intuition in Science

Medawar's third lecture "Mainly about Intuition" suggests that the true way of scientific research is what has come to be known as the hypothetico-deductive method. This takes the form of an exploratory dialogue, in which the two alternate voices are imaginative and critical. We have a problem to resolve: the *first* and creative step is to wonder if such and such might be the answer. Then we reason in our critical voice "Well, if it is so, then this should happen if we perform a particular experiment." If it doesn't we must start again with a fresh hunch; if it does, we can have tentative faith in our hypothesis, but it should be tested further. Note that although the critical phase uses logic, the imaginative phase is immediate and a-logical (not illogical, just something unrelated to logic). Also that the investigation does *not* start with observation or experiment, except for such preliminary soundings as may be made "to get the feel of the problem."

> The scientific method is a potentiation of common sense, . . . it can be resolved into a dialogue between fact and fancy, the actual and the possible; between what could be true and what is in fact the case.

This hypothetico-deductive scheme does measure up to the specification for a good methodology whereas the inductive method fails on every point.

Medawar argues his case in an especially compelling fashion, but (as he is at pains to point out) the basic ideas are by no means new. Indeed they have been around for well over a century, notably in the writings of Whewell, Mill, and Claude Bernard. Why then has the fiction about the inductive technique persisted for so long?

> Scientists are usually too proud or too shy to speak about creativity and "creative imagination"; they feel it to be incompatible with their conception of themselves as "men of facts" and rigorous inductive judgments.

True, but is there not also a half-conscious element of shame that the primary element in research is a mysterious process that is unpredictable, unreliable, and unbiddable, and that cannot be taught, though indeed it can be encouraged? In short, the principle at the very heart of scientific activity is itself "unscientific"!

Most scientists prefer not to think about this uncomfortable aspect of their work. Like religion, it is a subject one rarely talks about. This is a pity, for the workings of intuition need not remain "unscientific." It is disappointing that Medawar devotes only his last few pages to an analysis of the workings of intuition and a classification (which seems incomplete) of the ways in which it can manifest.

Why should scientists look askance at intuition or inspiration, when it is well recognized as a source of creative work in the arts? The hinted analogy with religion is not fanciful and should be acknowledged. Young scientists should be taught that there is a source beyond the normal workings of the mind of man from which inspiration may come, never on command but sometimes in response to a humble plea. Also that the practice of meditation can induce a receptive frame of mind. There have indeed been a few attempts along these lines. For the guidance of individuals, de Bono has written articles, and a book, on what he calls lateral thinking.[2] His advice is to cease from *direct* mental attack on a baffling problem and to think *around* it instead, widening the field over which the mind is allowed to roam. This calls for a relaxed frame of mind, but relaxation must not go so far as idle daydreaming, for one has to be alert to seize upon anything relevant that may slip into the receptive mind.

Research groups at some American universities have worked out a similar technique for use by groups, which they call brainstorming sessions. Members of the group must know and respect each other well enough to have confidence that all will obey the simple rules. These are that anyone should speak up the moment anything occurs to him that seems worth contributing. Then, however wild his ideas may sound, the others may not attack them destructively or scornfully. No comment is made unless the idea sparks off another brainwave. In successful sessions a temporary group consciousness may be established that is greater than the sum of the parts because a collective channel for inspiration is opened. Such a technique was used fruitfully in the more philosophical discussions that led to the writing of this book.

Related practices such as meditation, introspection, and contemplation may clear the way for the full mystical experience. The mind and emotions must first be cleared of trivial matters and composed—something that is already second nature to a scientist; then there must be yearning for enlightenment on some specific problem, or more often upon the mysteries of life in general. Meditation of this type, or prayer if one is inclined to religion, will promote mystical and illuminative experiences. There must also be a readiness to let go of self, one's yearning for wisdom being paramount. Yet this intensity of striving is liable to defeat its own object by leading to tension; only when it is released can consciousness slip into the wider realm. So such practices are more likely to prepare the way for a later experience, whether of full cosmic consciousness or some lesser ecstasy, at some moment when it is totally unexpected.

Intuitions can range in impact from the trivial to the world-shattering, from the felicitous phrase to use in a lecture or book to Einstein's Theory of Relativity. Despite the difference in intensity the quality of intuition remains unchanged; it comes as a sudden irruption into the mind, whole and fully fledged and often unexpectedly; it is received with a surge of joy, small or great. It appears to the recipient to be incontrovertibly true; but unfortunately experience shows that when put to practical test ideas derived from the intuition often prove to be wrong. Their source may be pure truth, but it is not conveyed in words or diagrams. As Emerson put it, "The soul answers never by words, but by the thing itself that is inquired after." Translation by the personal mind into rational thoughts that can be set down on paper can introduce distortion amounting even to falsification. Or, as in the hypothetico-deductive approach, the wrong hypothesis or specification may be presented, the wrong screen may be set up, and the response which comes, or seems to come, from the intuitional level does not square with the observed facts. Sometimes, too, an individual may believe he is inspired when he is only daydreaming his personal imaginings.

Whence comes intuition? From the unconscious mind, says the psychologist, as if that solved the mystery. But that merely suggests a location without solving the problem; how did the new creative idea get into the unconscious mind in the first place? The psychologist explains that it just shuffles around the facts already in its possession until they fall into a significant sequence. But this really won't do either, except for the more trivial intuitions, for this just brings us back again to inductivism, performed at the unconscious level. The worthwhile hypothesis is definitely something more than a classification of observed facts; it includes an original creative element, a new understanding that in most instances did not exist before in any human mind. Nothing less can account for the intense aesthetic satisfaction that accompanies a great intuition. This really cannot be explained without invoking some universal source of wisdom, of which fragments drop into prepared and receptive minds from time to time. Since the rest of this source is by definition still unknown, one can do no more than name it, as the Mind of Nature, Cosmic Intelligence, the Oversoul (Emerson), or God, as imagination suggests.

As suggested in Chapter 2, we may envisage an ocean of intelligence, within which individual human minds are immersed as somewhat loosely-enclosed portions of that ocean. A similar analogy is that of an iceberg, of which the visible tip represents the conscious mind, the greater submerged part the unconscious mind, the sea the collective unconscious and its depths Universal Intelligence. In this analogy (which must not be pushed too far) the individual minds are represented as crystallized out from, and appropriately a little more rigid and set than, the fluidic sea.

The Nature of Intuition

Many years ago, following Bergson's philosophy which was prominent at the time, Professor J. Emile Marcault developed Bergsonian ideas on the intuition in a little-known booklet on *The Psychology of Intuition* which was published in 1927.[3] Intuition, according to Marcault, is to be regarded as a faculty of a deeper or higher level of consciousness than that of the body and personality, the lower self of feeling and thought. This higher level of consciousness is still subjective for most people and this accounts for the mysterious nature of intuition.

> Reflection would be impossible did we not possess an objective field of consciousness wherein the objects of reflection reside, and a subjective self capable of reflecting upon it. Without such a structure, intuition, or the subjectivising of the self, could not take place.

The most fascinating feature of Marcault's exposition is the manner in which he expands and generalizes the concept of intuition. Instead of being limited to something that operates through the mind, as generally supposed, the influence of this intuitive faculty can irrupt into the normal levels at which consciousness functions, those of body, emotion, and mind, and lead to successive creative development of faculty at these various levels. Marcault's ideas seem worth quoting, though they are expressed in a more dogmatic, hard and fast style than is generally acceptable today. Moreover the ages that Marcault gave, nearly 50 years ago, may need revision, for it has been observed that many children now mature earlier. Also the stages he indicated are not really distinct steps, but more like phases in the expression of intuition and some children may take two or more concurrently rather than consecutively.

A method analogous to that of the mental tests used in schools, but applicable to all ages, enables us to detect "the plane of reflection or intuition"—that is the level in the hierarchy of functions where the diaphragm dividing the two selves is found. . . . From birth to five or six years of age intuition takes place at the level of *sensation*. All other functions being subjective, the absolute of self-consciousness endows sensorial intuition with that glory, that splendour, that sacredness which intuition always carries with it—the mark of the spiritual absolute. . . . From five to ten years intuition takes place at the level of the *activity* function. The child reflects on action, plans, executes, delights in adventure, imposes his creative energies, the absolute of his activity, on the outside world. "Make believe" is one manifestation of this absolute of action, one of the forms of this active intuition.

From ten to fourteen years (early adolescence) *emotion* becomes the seat of intuition—and should be the object of education. All other functions, whether already objectivised or still subjective, are then subservient to emotion, the logic of thought is placed at its service to justify the wish or ward off the cause of fear. . . . Only in the later adolescent period (thirteen to eighteen) does the intuition pass on to the *mind:* intellectual idealism replaces emotional idealism; the youth believes in ideas, in doctrines, in systems, delights in science, in dialectics, revels in abstractions.

In adult life intuition continues to evolve and manifests at the higher mind level of the social sense, expressed through idealistic political thinking, internationalism, and altruism of all kinds. Finally, intuition can function at its own level of the cosmic sense, corresponding to what has been termed cosmic consciousness or the mystical experience. Few people have yet reached this stage as an abiding state or frequent occurrence, but more have known it for brief unforgettable moments.

Backward individuals do not progress beyond an earlier stage in this expansion of intuition; in Marcault's terms the diaphragm dividing the two selves, or the objective and subjective aspects of consciousness, fails to rise beyond a certain level.

A characteristic feature of intuition, at whatever level, is that it is never at the command of the personal self. One does not really *have* an intuition; it always comes unbidden and without warning from "within" or "above," from subjective or unconscious levels, in a compelling fashion that seizes entire possession of the individual for as long as is needed, which may be only a moment. While the experience lasts it absorbs full attention and everything else is excluded. But when the full mystical experience occurs, at its own level of the cosmic sense, then it is one's very individuality that is excluded. The personal self suffers temporary eclipse as one is merged gloriously into universal consciousness. This is the experience some mystics have called "naughtedness" or entering the void. Thus one dies and becomes reborn, never to be quite the same as before.

Most Eastern religions recognize this state as the supreme achievement, variously known as Nirvana, Samadhi, Satori, and so on. In the Western world it has been experienced not only by Christian mystics, but also by many people not devoutly religious. Probably the first compilation of examples of what he called Cosmic Consciousness was made by Bucke from published sources and personal knowledge, in 1901.[4] A better-known one is William James's *Varieties of Religious Experience*. Among modern works, Marghanita Laski's *Ecstacy*[5] is confusing because it includes numerous examples of minor ecstacies, along with an extraordinarily detailed analysis of the characteristics of ecstacies great and small, and what may trigger them off. There is also a compilation of examples and analysis made by the physicist Raynor Johnson (*Watcher on the Hills*).[6]

The various types of yoga are designed to lead ultimately to union with the Supreme; yoga indeed means union. The koans of Zen Buddhism have the same objective; the seemingly nonsense questions force the consciousness into that realm where the pairs of opposites are transcended by deeper wisdom. There is no shortcut for the pleasure-seeking extrovert: those few to whom the mystical experience comes without deliberate preparation are individuals of a quiet, reflective, altruistic way of life. There are, however, crash techniques that may help in overcoming the last inhibitions that hold one back from letting go of self, to unite with the Self. But they work only for those who are already almost on the brink; for the unprepared they are ineffective and may be dangerous. One such technique is the use of hallucinogenic drugs such as LSD, which have undoubtedly brought meaningful experiences to some serious individuals—Aldous Huxley for example. But shallow persons experience only heightened sensory perceptions and fantasies, which are nearly as likely to be horrific as pleasurable. Occasionally, however, they enable a suitable person to have a brief experience which enlarges his whole attitude to life and living. Experiences of this nature are never forgotten. So strong are their effects on the mind and the personality that even errant behavior and habits can be permanently cured and a human life can be brought back to harmony by one short contact with this previously unrecognized inner world. Whether the use of hallucinogenic drugs will be finally vindicated in modern society will depend a great deal on the understanding and skill of those who select recipients and take on the responsibility of administering the right drug for that person, in the right quantity and under the right physical and psychological conditions. This problem has been discussed by Stafford and Golightly, who plead for relaxation of laws which hamper even medicinal use of these drugs in many countries.[7]

Another technique for helping to concentrate awareness inwardly is simply to remove external stimuli. Sensory deprivation has been applied in psychological studies by confining subjects wearing blindfolds, earplugs, and thick gloves in small soundproof rooms. Until recently such investigations have revealed only undesirable effects; the college students generally used as subjects have experienced visual and auditory hallucinations (with an occasional veridical psychic experience), and a day of this may drive

them to the verge of insanity. It was recently found, however, that subjects brought up in relatively solitary conditions on remote Norwegian farms were unaffected by
sensory deprivation and just pondered on their work.[8]
Thus for alert town-dwellers normally exposed to almost
continuous sensory stimulus, total isolation proved catastrophic; for agricultural workers accustomed to peace
and quiet it was merely neutral; but the psychologists for-
got the age-old knowledge that for the yogi it can be of positive value, when he retires to his quiet mountain cave or
monastic cell for undisturbed meditation.

Thus the normal sense channels and the rational mind
can be bypassed and direct knowledge can be gained by intuition and the mystical experience. There are some who
claim that the normal channels can be bypassed in another
fashion, by extrasensory perception (ESP). This involves
the so-called psychic mode of consciousness—and we are
all psychic to some extent. The psychic obtains information in a way which appears (to the psychic) to be objective
but which others would probably define as subjective.
However, there is no hard and fast dividing line between
the psychic person—constantly exhibiting extrasensory
perception, more or less at will—and "normal" individuals, in which psychic information appears rather more
rarely, and usually in ways different from those in which
they appear to the psychic person. Few people have the
psychic senses at their command; for most, the experiences
come erratically without conscious volition.

Mystical experience is incommunicable; psychic experience can certainly be communicated (described) but sometimes it has to be "interpreted." Very often the psychic will
see a symbol which conveys to him a clear message; at other
times the message is not nearly so clear and must be interpreted, with much cogitation. The nonpsychic person will
usually receive such symbols in the form of dreams (the
stock in trade of the psychoanalyst); sometimes the symbols
will break through into the waking consciousness, when
the individual is in a state of mental relaxation or tranquil-
lity, or at other times in a state of extreme stress and
concentration.

In trying to understand this, it is helpful to recall the analogy suggested earlier between the human mind and an iceberg. The portion above the sea is the conscious mind. The part below the sea is the unconscious mind. The sea itself is the collective unconscious. In the depths of the sea are the mystical levels of experience. The analogical picture is inverted—the heights of consciousness are represented by the depths of the sea. All knowledge is there: the mind at its deepest level is perhaps in full knowledge of everything in the universe. But between these depths and conscious knowledge stands the personal unconscious, and on its way through this the uprising intuitions become changed into symbols. Any item of knowledge that has a psychic "energy level" sufficient for the individual concerned can find its way through to the conscious mind, crystallizing appropriate imagery on the way, for presentation to the conscious mind. In some examples no imagery is produced but the autonomic nervous system is caused to move muscles, as in automatic writing and water divining.

Telepathy is another form of ESP which occurs rather frequently between some individuals who are emotionally close to one another, and which has been the subject of innumerable experiments. Such direct communication is not too difficult to understand, in general terms, in the light of the hypothesis that individual minds are immersed in a universal mind; it is then only necessary for the insubstantial barriers around individual minds to be penetrated.

The conscious mind normally receives experiences only from the physical world, and so the information rising into the conscious mind from the unconscious must simulate physical forms. The unconscious deals in symbols. The mystic may see a vision of the Christ, or of the Buddha, in the traditional form. The medium may see a shadowy representation of the physical body of the deceased person (his symbol). Sometimes the symbols will take the form of other archetypes such as the mandala. With the symbol will come often a voice, speaking in words understood by the percipient, or sometimes a scent which may recall a memory. The symbols of the psychic levels of the mind are often the vehicle for truth. Sometimes their meaning is clear; at other times a story is woven around them, and its meaning has to be unraveled later. But always the visions, the dreams, appear objective. The visions of the psychic are glimpses into the psychic world—the mind level dealing with desire, emotion, symbolism. This is the world we all find ourselves in immediately after death (and sometimes during sleep), and the experiences we have of this world in waking life may sometimes be caused by our friends and acquaintances in that world. But the psychic world is a world of illusion: our experiences of it are not always veridical. It is a world of wish-fulfillment, a maya, an illusion, in which "under every flower a serpent lies coiled." It is the symbols of this mental-emotional world which appear in consciousness in extrasensory perception.

It is important to appreciate the degrees of objectivity and subjectivity of the different levels of consciousness of a human being. To a normal average conscious person the physical world is a world of complete objectivity—it is *given*—whereas the emotional-mental world of the psychic is a world of complete subjectivity. This may not be at all a true view. The physical world as we each consider we know it—a world of objects of various kinds—is actually nowhere but in our own minds, in the form that we apprehend it. It is only approximately the same world as "seen" by others, in their minds. As has been mentioned earlier (Chapter 1), each of us has direct "experiential knowledge," and from this we *postulate* the physical world. Those objects around us are items of "the rational component of knowledge." We explain the differences between our individual postulated physical worlds by such expressions as "he is color blind," "she is seeing an illusion." However, by and large, there do not appear to be very great differences in our various subjectively perceived physical worlds, so most of us accept that they are representations of a real world. At the other end of the perceptivity spectrum the mystic experiences a quite different world in which he and the rest of the universe are one. All knowledge (of the eternal verities) seems to be his. Past, present, and future are merged into the "eternal now." In between those two limits are various degrees of objectivity and subjectivity. The mental-emotional world immediately next to the physical appears to have some "objectivity," some *givenness,* but not nearly so much as has the physical world. It seems to be a world rather like the physical but functioning according to the laws of psychology rather than the laws of physics. It is like the physical because it seems to be constructed in an automatic way from our memories of the physical world and our desires, both conscious and unconscious. Information coming from this world of the shallow unconscious may be true; the information could be coming from the deeper, truly intuitive, levels only a little short of the deepest levels of the mystical experience. But it could be false—it may be what we *wish* were true—created by ourselves at the mental-emotional level. And again it could be partially true, partially false, for it may be information from deeper levels, colored by our own desires or fears.

How can we distinguish what is true and what is false—and what is partially true? This question arises whenever we think we have a "true" intuition, just as it arises when we wonder whether the results of extrasensory perception have validity. We can find the truth only by testing it against every valid standard. Sometimes what is thought to be a real intuition will be proved counterfeit by such tests. Perhaps, as we develop in perception and understanding of these inner realms, the "truths" which reach us as the result of both the operations of intuition and extrasensory perception will prove to be more often true. Perhaps intuition and ESP will grow together and become one. These objectives will be advanced by appropriate self-training and self-discipline, directed for example to avoiding confused emotional states, thinking clearly and exactly, and learning to still the mind. Some suitable techniques are presented by Christmas Humphreys in his book, *Western Approach to Zen.*[9] Then the stilled mind will respond increasingly accurately to extrasensory perception. The less personally identified we are with the confused self-interested and conditioned thought patterns of our *personal* minds the better will we be able to receive true intuitions, and register extrasensory percepts.

As the great psychologist C.G. Jung says in his autobiography, "Everything in the unconscious seeks outward manifestation, and the personality too desires to evolve out of its unconscious conditions and to experience itself as a whole." Perhaps the purpose of our life, of our evolutionary development, is to make the unconscious conscious. In the unconscious is all Truth.

Summary

The rational mind, whether it operates by inductive or deductive reasoning, is not the only route to truth. Through the ages enlightened men and women have recognized a more direct and immediate approach, namely intuition. It is an elusive faculty that can be wooed and encouraged, but not commanded. When one is seized by an intuition all else is momentarily excluded, and the revelation bears the imprint of undeniable truth. It can, however, become distorted and falsified when it is brought down to the rational level and expressed in words. Few scientists have acknowledged or studied the operation of intuition, though it is clear that all truly creative workers in science and the arts rely upon it. It is suggested that intuition represents brief communion with Cosmic Intelligence. The mystical experience or cosmic consciousness appears to represent a more complete immersion in this Universal Mind. The various types of extrasensory perception represent additional routes to truth though at present somewhat unreliable ones.

REFERENCES

[1] P.B. Medawar, *Induction and Intuition in Scientific Thought*, Methuen, University Paperback, London, 1969.

[2] E. de Bono, *The Use of Lateral Thinking*, Jonathan Cape, London.

[3] J.E. Marcault, *The Psychology of Intuition*, Theosophical Publishing House, London, 1927.

[4] R.M. Bucke, Cosmic Consciousness, E.P. Dutton & Co., New York, 4th ed., 1923.

[5] Marghanita Laski, *Ecstasy*, The Cresset Press of London, 1961.

[6]Raynor C. Johnson, *Watcher on the Hills*, Hodder & Stoughton, London, 1959.

[7]P.G. Stafford and B.H. Golightly, *LSD in Action*, Sidgwick & Jackson, London, 1969.

[8]E.A. Haggard *et al. Journal of Abnormal Psychology*, 1970, *76*, 1.

[9]Christmas Humphreys, *Western Approach to Zen*, Allen and Unwin, London, 1972.

Section Two

THE ORIGIN OF LIFE ON EARTH

CHAPTER 7

THE MATERIALS OF LIFE

The previous chapters have discussed some of the ways in which intelligence shows itself in man. Self-consciousness and the ability to perform intelligent action are inescapable aspects of our everyday experience, just as certain to us as our possession of bodies composed of physical matter. Thus any theory which seeks to explain the emergence of biological life on the planet must also explain convincingly the appearance of intelligence and consciousness.

This chapter explains briefly how chemical substances that comprise the building blocks from which living forms are constructed may have arisen initially on the earth. The following chapter reviews hypotheses that have attempted the much more difficult task of accounting for the infusion of biological life into these inert substances to bring about the emergence of primitive living forms. When pressed to their biological conclusions can such hypotheses support the concept, widely accepted by scientists, that matter is primal and that life and intelligence are secondarily derived functions? Or shall we be driven to conclude that they cannot stand up to such close scrutiny, so that we are compelled to accept the alternative hypothesis that life, intelligence, and consciousness are the primal realities, and that their expression in biological forms on earth is the secondary event?

Plants and animals are composed of a characteristic range of chemical substances. These are compounds of carbon (C) with hydrogen (H), oxygen (O), and often nitrogen (N), sometimes including phosphorus (P) or sulphur (S) and less frequently a number of other essential elements. At one time it was believed that these were specifically biological molecules that could be elaborated only by living organisms. The first step in disproving this hypothesis was taken in 1828 by Wohler, who synthesized urea very simply by heating ammonium cyanate, when the atoms of C, H, O, and N rearranged themselves into a new pattern. Since then organic chemists have synthesized biological molecules of ever increasing complexity, including even vitamins and small proteins and nucleic acids. These have been built up from simpler substances and ultimately from inorganic compounds or right from the elements. However, the synthetic techniques are often complicated, requiring special reagents and solvents and sometimes elevated temperatures or pressures; so there did not seem to be much scope for the elaboration of such molecules in inorganic nature, in the sea and the lakes for example, at ambient temperatures and pressures in dilute aqueous solution. Until recently, therefore, the occurrence of complex organic substances, in petroleum for example or in meteorites, was accepted as evidence of biological origin.

Biologists were thus faced with the fundamental version of the old joke: Which came first, the chicken or the egg? When living creatures, presumably single-celled microorganisms, first arose on the primitive earth, what was there to eat if their food could be synthesized only by living organisms?

Synthesis under Reducing Conditions

A way round this dilemma arose from theories about conditions on the primitive earth, which were probably entirely different from those of today. It is generally believed that the atmosphere was then reducing rather than oxidizing, containing gases like ammonia and lower hydrocarbons in place of oxygen. Also the earth was probably more violent in those times, with local hot areas due to volcanoes and geysers, and more storms with lightning. Besides these energy sources to promote chemical reactions, it is likely that more ultraviolet radiation from the sun reached the earth because it was less effectively screened by the primitive atmosphere than by the present one containing ozone, which absorbs the ultraviolet light.

In the 1920s A. Oparin in Russia and J.B.S. Haldane in England published speculations about the origin of life, but it is only in the last two decades that a new branch of chemistry has arisen that sets out to discover what organic molecules are synthesized under simulated primitive earth conditions. This is called prebiotic or abiotic synthesis, i.e. the formation of organic molecules in the absence of life. It started with S. Miller in 1953, and the work has been continued by P. Abelson, J. Oro, S. Fox, L. Orgel, and others.[1-6]

Such investigations are, of course, intensely speculative. It is unlikely that we shall ever know the exact composition of the atmosphere several thousand million years ago; it is generally agreed that it was reducing in nature, though even this basic assumption has recently been queried. Anyhow, plausible mixtures of gases such as methane (CH_4), ammonia (NH_3), and water vapor have been subjected for many hours to heat, sunlight, ultraviolet light, ionizing radiations, or electrical discharges by spark or arc, sometimes with crushed rocks added as natural catalysts. Finally, the tarry product of the witches' brew had to be separated into its numerous components by modern analytical techniques. The list of organic substances produced in these ways has rapidly expanded; it now includes sugars, fatty acids, bases, and most of the amino acids in present-day proteins, sometimes free, sometimes already linked into small peptides. (See Chapter 9 for a description of amino acids and proteins.)

Until recently two types of compounds essential to life resisted synthesis by these prebiotic methods. The first were the sulphur-containing amino acids, but now traces of the most important one, methionine, have been identified after irradiating with ultraviolet light a mixture containing ammonium thiocyanate, a compound of N, H, S, C and O. The latter compound is a legitimate starting material, for it has been found in volcanic gases, arising from the combination of carbon dioxide, hydrogen sulphide and ammonia. The second were compounds related to the chlorophyll of green plants (porphyrins) that can act as catalysts; they are important because they can harness the abundant energy of sunlight in the visible part of the spectrum to promote synthesis of organic compounds.

Polymerization

Most of the substances produced by prebiotic or abiotic synthesis are relatively small molecules. But living cells are mainly composed of very large molecules (polymers) like proteins, polysaccharides (e.g. starch and cellulose) and nucleic acids (see Chapter 9). These arise by condensation of numerous similar molecules into long chains, with elimination of a molecule of water between each pair (condensation or dehydration reactions). Now it is intrinsically unlikely that such reactions involving loss of water would occur in an environment that mainly consisted of water; indeed it would be more likely to promote in the course of time the reverse reactions, namely hydrolysis (i.e. addition of water) to convert the polymers back into their constituents. Therefore supplementary reaction conditions have been invoked to bring about the condensation reactions. Professor Sidney Fox and his group at the University of Miami have shown that mixtures of amino acids react to form protein-like molecules called proteinoids simply by heating them dry at temperatures above the boiling point of water.[7] It can be imagined that pools of water containing primitive amino acids were dried out by the sun or by volcanic heat and that the dried residues became heated sufficiently by either agency before they were washed away by rain.

Another possibility is alternate freezing and thawing of a lake in winter and summer. As pure ice separated out, the dissolved substances would remain in the diminishing amount of liquid water until eventually the solution became so concentrated that condensation reactions could occur. Recent studies at the Salk Institute[5] have shown that such conditions could yield purines, constituents of the vital nucleic acids of the cell nucleus. They could arise from hydrocyanic acid (HCN), likely to be present in the primitive atmosphere, in two steps. It would dissolve in the lake water and self-condensation could occur in the concentrated solution left when the lake froze nearly solid. Then, in summer, ultraviolet light could convert the resulting intermediate into purines.

Another agency that has been invoked to promote condensation reactions is the tides. Sea water would wash back and forth over rocks on the foreshore and, as first suggested by J.D. Bernal,[8] dissolved substances would be taken up (adsorbed) onto certain minerals, in particular apatite; then when the tide receded, these rocks would be heated up by the sun, and this could promote reactions between the adsorbed substances. This notion was formulated more precisely by a team at the University of Rochester, New York, and is strongly supported by their experimental findings.[9] The mineral apatite, a form of calcium phosphate, forms crystals with minute grooves on their surfaces within which many molecules can be selectively adsorbed from solution and aligned in such a manner as to promote their interaction at moderately elevated temperatures. The common amino acids found in proteins are nearly all bound by apatite to some degree, and future work may reveal conditions under which they will combine to form peptides. More important, possibly, is the finding that certain inorganic and organic compounds containing phosphorus are strongly bound so that conditions exist for the synthesis of some key molecules of biochemistry. These include the nucleotides that make up nucleic acids (see Chapter 9) and adenosine triphosphate, an important catalyst that can cause polymerizations of simple molecules into larger ones more typical of living cells.

Thus there are grounds for supposing that numerous organic substances became present in the "primeval soup." Moreover, it appears that the range of substances produced under simulated primitive earth conditions is similar whichever energy source is used; it is also noteworthy that many of the compounds are precisely those that occur predominantly in living organisms. So if events really did occur in this fashion in the "primeval soup," then the stage was set for the emergence of primitive life.

But as the next chapter will show, there were difficulties, and the appearance of life could not have been so inevitable and automatic as some authorities seem to believe.

Summary

It is believed that the atmosphere on the primitive earth was devoid of oxygen. Simulated reducing atmospheres have been subjected to various energy sources, heat, light, and other radiations, and numerous organic molecules have been detected in the resulting tarry products. Plausible conditions probably existed on the primitive earth under which these products of abiotic synthesis could polymerize into the larger molecules more typical of living organisms, thus setting the stage for the emergence of life.

REFERENCES

[1] S.L. Miller, *Science*, 1953, *117*, 528.

[2] P.H. Abelson, Paleobiochemistry, in *Evolutionary Biochemistry*, ed. A.I. Oparin et al., 1963, Pergamon Press, London.

[3] J. Oro, *Nature*, 1961, *190*, 389.

[4] S.W. Fox, ed. *The Origins of Prebiological Systems; and Their Molecular Structure*, Academic Press, New York, 1965.

[5] R. Sanchez, J. Ferris, and L. Orgel, *J. Molec. Biol.*, 1967, *30*, 233.

[6] C. Ponnamperuma, *Nature*, 1964, *201*, 337. *Origins of Life*, Thames and Hudson, London, 1972.

[7] S.W. Fox and K. Harada, *J. Am. Chem. Soc.*, 1960, *82*, 3745.

[8] J.D. Bernal, *The Origin of Life*, Weidenfeld and Nicolson, London, 1967.

[9] M.W. Neuman, W.F. Neuman, and K. Lane, *Currents in Modern Biology*, 1970, *3*, 253 & 277.

CHAPTER 8

THE COMING OF LIFE

The stage was set for the *spontaneous automatic* emergence of life; or was it? Certainly there are biologists who believe this to be so, claiming the work on prebiotic synthesis as sufficient evidence. "In the beginning life assembled itself" was the confident title of a paper by Sidney Fox in *New Scientist*.[1] But there are others who cannot bring themselves to gloss over the insuperable difficulties; for them, the emergence of life is not merely a puzzle but also a great mystery. Half a century ago there was more excuse for believing in the automatic emergence of life, for microorganisms appeared at that time to be mere blobs of protoplasm. The recently discovered colloidal state was invoked to "explain" life; and droplets called coacervates, that sometimes separate from mixtures of colloids and bear superficial resemblance to bacteria, were regarded as a sort of half-way stage to living organisms. But biochemistry has since shown that "protoplasm" (a term no longer used) comprises a staggering array of complex organic substances with highly specific functions. Also advances in microscopy, especially electron microscopy, have revealed highly organized structures within even the smallest bacteria and algae, and even in the still smaller viruses. Thus the more we learn the more difficult it becomes to imagine that objects of such complexity could have assembled themselves without intelligent guidance. Yet some scientists remain so obsessed by materialistic mechanisms that they still cling to the idea of spontaneous generation.

Spontaneous Generation

The attitude has changed over the centuries. In earlier times it was taken for granted that creatures emerged naturally from organic materials. The alchemist van Helmont even published a recipe for producing mice artificially by leaving damp grain and dirty rags in a covered vessel. But as early as 1660 Redi demonstrated that no maggots appeared in rotten meat if it was covered with fine gauze to keep the flies off. The idea of spontaneous generation gradually lost credibility but was revived in respect of microorganisms by Leeuwenhoek's discovery in the seventeenth century of the microscopic "infusoria" that appeared in vegetable broths and pond water. It was not until the middle of the nineteenth century that Pasteur finally convinced the scientific world that such broths could be sterilized by heat and kept sterile so long as they were sealed or exposed only to filtered air. But then, a century later, the idea was revived again, with the difference that spontaneous generation was only to be expected in a reducing atmosphere. It now appears that some people who are recreating prebiotic soups, half expect them to come to life one of these days. If the idea were really credible, the consequences could be very disturbing. There appears to be lack of coordination between academic disciplines here, for the whole science of bacteriology is founded upon the assumption that spontaneous generation never occurs. This is well supported by the millions of tubes of culture media, both aerobic and anaerobic, that have remained sterile in the absence of deliberate infection, even though such media are richer in nutrients than the prebiotic soups. In addition there are the thousands of millions of cans of edible soup and other foods, which we hope to find sterile on opening. It is suggested that new life can arise only under anaerobic reducing conditions; but presumably suitable conditions exist in faulty canned foods when attack on the iron has occurred, leading to "hydrogen swells." It would not be scientific to suggest that what happened of itself on the primitive earth could not happen today, and indeed Bernal specifically rejects the idea. "If life once made itself, it must not be too difficult to make it again."[2] So those who seriously believe in spontaneous generation should surely have enough faith in their convictions to search for new forms of life in modern nourishing soups rather than in simulated prebiotic ones. They should be begging for culture media and canned foods that show unexpected signs of life normally attributed to faulty sterilization.

Some seek escape from such uncomfortable consequences in the notion that it may have taken millions of years for life to arise in some gradual fashion. Such a notion may have its origin in a subconscious illogical hope that, given long enough, the inconceivable might happen, for it can draw no support from biochemistry. Long periods are indeed needed to produce biologically useless products like coal. But that order of time does not really help for creating the first microorganism, for its first ordered moiety would fall apart again or decompose long before the rest were built up if it took so long. So unless one can envisage some kind of prebiotic memory code for the continual rebuilding of molecular aggregates destined to prove useful in the distant future, the whole task must have been accomplished within a relatively short time. The alternative of colonization of the planet with organisms from outer space—the old panspermia idea—no longer appears so impossible as it did at one time, but relegates the problem of the origin of life to a more distant time and place.

Creation of Primitive Organisms

There is little doubt that the primaeval soup could nourish primitive organisms once they had arisen on the earth. Numerous microorganisms thrive in the very dilute culture medium of present-day lakes and oceans, without benefit of photosynthetic abilities. But this is altogether different from the problem of assembling *ab initio* the body of even the most primitive organism imaginable. This is something that is still a long way from being possible even with all the resources of modern science and human skill. Moreover, even supposing it were ever possible to assemble correctly all the component parts of a simple organism, what reason is there to suppose that it would suddenly come alive? Is it not much more probable that it would just remain a nonliving replica of an entity? So is it likely that blind chance could do better, even given aeons of time? Because there are those who profess to believe that the answer is yes, it is necessary to spell out some of the difficulties.

Living organisms can utilize the most improbable substances as food because they are able to transform them, with the help of a battery of enzymes, into the specific compounds they need for cellular growth and reproduction. But to build up the initial primary organism every one of the many thousands of these specific compounds must be available ready-made. The substances presumed from simulation experiments to exist on the primitive earth are mostly no more than crude models for such specific compounds; they have the wrong composition and the wrong shape. Biological proteins, for example, may contain hundreds of amino acids, linked together in a single chain (sometimes two or more) in a highly specific order. The positions of cysteine molecules in the chain determine the sites at which sulphur bridges can occur. These, and the attractions and repulsions between water-attracting and water-repelling side chains on some of the constituent amino acids, determine the tertiary structure of the molecule, i.e. the way it coils and folds in three-dimensional space. Modern research is showing that it is precisely this tertiary structure that enables the protein to perform its particular function, as an enzyme or the oxygen-carrying hemoglobin for example. As it happens, the compositions and three-dimensional structures of hemoglobins from a number of species have been determined in detail. They all have almost exactly the same shape, and their compositions differ only to the extent of substitutions of one amino acid for another one here and there in the molecule; these variations do not occur close to the active site and are such as not to alter the tertiary structure or overall shape appreciably.

It is not suggested that primeval organisms used hemoglobin, but they must have needed enzymes, and similar work has revealed that these are just about as exacting in their formulation. The variants that occur, between species and sometimes within a species, similarly involve relatively few amino acids situated moreover away from the active site at which the enzymic reaction occurs. Compare these molecules with the proteinoids produced by simulated prèbiotic synthesis. These are indeed not utterly random since their overall composition differs from that of the amino acid mixture used to make them. Nevertheless it is extremely improbable that all the proteinoid molecules from a reaction mixture are identical, and more likely on the contrary that hardly any two are alike. Moreover they are nearly certain to contain tangled branched chains, like most synthetic polymers, instead of the unbranched chains typical of biological proteins. How can anyone imagine, if he really stops to think about it, that these nearly random polymers could serve even the most primitive organisms? To live at all these creatures must have been able to carry out at least some of the thousands of chemical reactions that proceed in modern microorganisms, where each reaction now requires a precision made enzyme molecule.

Stereochemistry

Nor is this the whole problem; the shape or configuration in three-dimensional space of organic molecules is determined in part by the stereochemistry of carbon compounds. So it is necessary to digress briefly to explain this topic. The carbon atom has four valencies or combining links, normally directed from the center to the corners of a regular tetrahedron. When linked to four *different* atoms or groups, the carbon atom is said to be asymmetric; the resulting molecule exists in two isomeric stereochemical forms, one of which is the mirror image of the other, though they are otherwise identical in chemical and physical properties. One of the simplest examples is the amino acid alanine, the two forms of which are illustrated in the diagram.

A chemical reaction always produces the two isomers in equal amounts, a so-called racemic mixture. The two

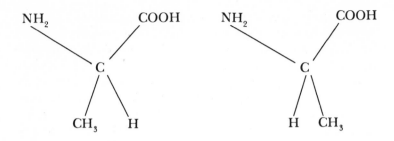

isomers rotate the plane of polarized light in opposite directions, which is why they are often called dextro and laevo (d and l or right and left) optical isomers. Although a racemic mixture is optically inactive, because the equal number of d and l molecules cancel each other out, an individual stereoisomer can be produced by some reaction that involves linkage to an existing asymmetric molecule. Alternatively the racemic mixture may be combined with, say, the laevo isomer of some already asymmetric substance, to form an ester for example; the resulting dl and ll compounds no longer have the mirror image relationship and will differ in some physical property such as solubility, so that they may be separable by fractional crystallization. Or again a yeast or other organism may be set to eat up the l form and leave the unnatural d isomer. Rarely, the stereoisomers of a racemic mixture may form crystals with right and left hand faces which can be recognized and separated by hand. It was this phenomenon, displayed by tartaric acid, that led Pasteur to the discovery of stereoisomerism. Complex molecules can exhibit multiple stereoisomerism and other forms of the phenomenon, but the principle persists. Generally speaking, whenever any carbon compound with asymmetric carbon atoms is produced *biologically* it occurs in only one of the possible stereoisomeric forms, usually that known as the l form.

Reverting to proteins, since each of the twenty or so natural amino acids contains an asymmetric carbon atom (except the simplest, glycine) biological proteins consist usually of chains of laevo amino acids. Naturally this stereochemical configuration affects their shape in three-dimensional space, so it is a factor in the determination of their tertiary structure and hence of their biological activity. An enzyme molecule in which even a few of the constituent amino acids had the wrong, or d, configuration would certainly have diminished activity or none at all. Now abiotic synthesis, whether under primitive earth conditions or with all the modern refinements of organic chemistry, always gives rise to racemic mixtures of isomers of any asymmetric carbon compound. In consequence, if optical activity were detected in any product, such as petroleum for example, or the organic matter from a carbonaceous meteorite, this would until recently have been regarded as infallible evidence of biological origin. Digressing, it may be mentioned that intense argument has indeed raged over the minute optical activity claimed for extracts of the Orgueil meteorite which contained structures believed by some to be those of fossil microorganisms from outer space. Disappointingly, it is now generally thought that the structures are of purely mineral origin and that the observed optical rotation is due to experimental error or to terrestrial contamination, for example by sweat from human fingers. In any event, it has recently been stated[3] that stereoisomers become comletely racemised, with corresponding loss of optical activity, in about 100,000 years. This calls for the reversal of earlier views, for it means that detection of optical activity in a meteorite extract is almost certain evidence of contamination; the only alternative is the unlikely assumption that the meteorite bore living organisms during the last 10,000 years or so.

The situation is more definite in respect of the Murchison meteorite, which fell in Australia in 1969.[4] It contains traces of half a dozen amino acids, which were fractionated by gas chromatography of derivatives, an extremely sensitive technique that can also distinguish between d and l isomers without polarimetry. Most of the amino acids present were dl mixtures; the slight excess of l form in some was probably due to contamination. Moreover two amino acids were present that are not found in natural proteins but can be made abiotically, i.e. in the absence of living organisms. From this and supporting evidence it was concluded that all the amino acids arose by abiotic synthesis in outer space—not so surprising as it would once have seemed, for a number of small carbon compounds have recently been detected in space.

Reverting, stereochemical configuration poses another "chick and egg" problem. We do not know any way by which natural l isomers could have been separated from the primeval soup except by living organisms, yet on the other hand the organisms could not be produced without them. It is a problem that all who support spontaneous generation ignore or dismiss unsatisfactorily; Bernal, for example, accords it only one page of his 340-page book, already cited.[2]

Stages in the Origin of Life

In that book Bernal faces the difficulties with great courage and explicitness yet manages to emerge undaunted by them all. He perceives three stages in the origin of life, namely:

1. Abiotic formation of simple organic compounds.
2. Formation of polymers, including specific polymers able in some unknown way to replicate themselves. This is described as chemical evolution and it might be proper to regard this stage as the beginning of life, in preorganismal form.
3. Formation of living organisms.

Bernal does at least formulate the necessary second stage, which is usually ignored. It involves a process remotely resembling crystallization, but differs profoundly in that it calls for the assemblage of *dissimilar* molecules into *specific linear* polymers. It is difficult to imagine this happening spontaneously even without the added problem of self-replication. Bernal is quite unable to suggest any convincing mechanism. Indeed, in the book as a whole, and within each section, the argument goes round in a circle. Life must have begun spontaneously and automatically; it is very hard to see how this came about and the more we know of biology and molecular biology the more difficult it seems. So God knows how it happened, but it did! Bernal derides faith as wishful thinking, yet he himself displays unshakable faith in what his entire book shows to be impossible. Yet here and there he absent-mindedly drops his guard and writes something that is tantamount to conceding defeat.

> All living things . . . carry in themselves their whole past and are not fully intelligible apart from their ancestry. This extended time requirement of all living things is the real characteristic of life which distinguishes it from the inorganic world. The structures life gives rise to, including the organisms themselves, are more expressions of this inner, prescribed molecular character of life. Indeed, as we see it now, the notion of *prescription* is the unique characteristic of life on the earth.

But prescription implies intelligence or information, and as Thorpe has shown, it cannot be inscribed in the material substance of atoms. So in effect we are asked to discard the Creator, or the Great Planner of some Western philosophers, in favor of an impersonal intelligence that prescribes the evolution of life. This notion is indeed entirely acceptable, though it goes beyond what Bernal himself intended.

Role of Chance

It is possible to make some calculations to illustrate the probability of the specific polymers required for life to arise by chance. This has been attempted for example, by F.B. *Salisbury*.[5] In order to follow this approach some familiarity with the concept of the genetic code is needed. This is outlined in Chapter 9 of this book, but at this point it suffices to state that genetic information is coded in the form of sequences of nucleotides making up the familiar self-replicating double helix of DNA (deoxyribonucleic acid). A sequence of three nucleotides is the code for a particular amino acid, and a length of DNA constituting a gene is the code for a complete protein, such as, for example, an enzyme able to carry out a specific reaction in the cell. A small enzyme molecule would contain some 300 amino acids, so the gene controlling its synthesis needs to comprise a chain of around 1,000 nucleotides. Now each nucleotide in the chain represents one of only four possibilities, but the right choice has to be made for every one of the one thousand links if the whole gene is to have the correct sequence. Thus for one link the probability is 1 in 4; for two links it is 1 in 4^2 or 1 in 16; for three links it is 1 in 4^3 or 1 in 64, so the probability becomes rapidly smaller as the number of links increases, and for a thousand links it is the unthinkably large number of 4^{1000} or about 10^{600} (i.e. the number 1 followed by 600 noughts). In other words, 10^{600} different DNA molecules each containing 1,000 nucleotides are theoretically possible but only one of them has the unique structure that codes for the specific protein. Actually some of the variants might produce slightly different proteins that would still retain at least a part of their function. Suppose even so many as 10^{100} variants would serve, which is equivalent to postulating that 166 out of the 1,000 nucleotides might be changed without the enzyme losing all its activity, then the probability is still only 1 in 10^{500}. As Salisbury points out, the entire universe (assumed to have a diameter of 20 thousand million light years) is not nearly large enough to contain so many DNA molecules even packed solid into the whole of space! Nor would there have been time during the entire existence of the earth as a planet, for so many molecules to have been produced. There is also the little problem of how the right one got sorted out for use, from a universe-sized heap of useless ones.

Yet these calculations concern only one protein out of the many kinds needed by the most primitive organism. It also takes no account of the complexity of the mechanism for translating the genetic code into protein. As described in later chapters, the process involves intermediate transcription onto RNA (ribonucleic acid) molecules; then the actual building of the protein chain is performed, with the help of a battery of enzymes, upon highly complex organelles within the cell known as ribosomes. Bernal recognizes in his book the impossibility of specific DNA molecules arising by chance, and even ridicules those who assume that life began with such molecules:

The picture of the solitary molecule of DNA on a primitive sea shore generating the rest of life was put forward with slightly less plausibility than that of Adam and Eve in the garden. The source of this implausibility of the DNA molecule as the origin of life was, in fact, because it had no obvious predecessor. Before being able to think of how the DNA molecule could give rise to organisms, it was necessary to ask how it got there in the first place.

Once the concept of the double helix DNA molecule carrying the genetic code was formulated it was almost universally taken for granted that proteins always had been built up by transcription from DNA. It is ironical that the protagonists of spontaneous generation thus made things unnecessarily difficult for themselves. Hardly any of them suggested that primitive organisms might have got by with less sophisticated mechanisms; but evidence has lately come to hand that certain bacteria still make some of their peptides (small proteins) by a simple enzyme mechanism not involving DNA. It is therefore reasonable to suppose that they have inherited this ability from the earliest forms of life. This simplification by no means implies that life could have started by chance, for innumerable other difficulties persist; it merely obviates some of the more ludicrous flights of imagination like those castigated by Salisbury.

Role of Prescription

As noted already, even Bernal rejects the pure chance hypothesis and proposes chemical evolution and prescription as vaguely formulated alternatives. "In other words, all the patterns of life are not planned, as we plan a machine or a work of art, on the basis of an idea or a model; but *prescribed* along various operational prescriptions which do not involve knowledge of the final product." But according to dictionary definitions, to prescribe is "to lay down as a rule," or "to lay down authoritatively for direction." These actions unavoidably imply intelligence, which indeed may not envisage the end product (as Bernal insists) but which does lay down the appropriate next steps. We may put it differently and suggest that Life, in the sense of disembodied intelligence, came first. Taken in *this* sense we may accept Fox's dictum "in the beginning life assembled itself." It had the problem of assembling the chemical atoms into molecules suitable for use by biological organisms (Bernal's chemical evolution) and then assembling these molecules into living entities. This usage of the word Life has been avoided in the rest of the book because it is contradictory in scientific terminology, in which "life" signifies exclusively biological life, and excludes the "life of the spirit" referred to by Christians. It is for this reason that the term "intelligence" has been adopted.

At the present stage of knowledge, little more than speculation about mechanisms is possible. An idea put forward by B. Butterworth[6] may however be helpful. He suggests that "life is as different from energy as energy is different from matter, and that life can interact with energy, as energy interacts with matter, without appearing *as* a form of energy." The change of mass is far too small to detect when a material such as petrol produces energy by combustion, so Einstein's famous equation $e=mC^2$ could not be derived or checked in this direct way. There may be a similarly infinitesimal difference between the input and output energies of a living organism representing the interaction of life, and the suggested relationship may not be denied simply because the energy difference is too small to detect. It remains the difficult task of science to try to discover the precise manner in which biological life was guided to emerge on earth; but at least it is a more hopeful task than trying to imagine how something happened that never could have happened, namely the emergence of life by pure chance. (See also Chapter 14.)

Some recent correspondence in *Nature* is relevant. In an editorial[7] this journal complained that "Fundamentalists on the Board of Education in California have argued that the teaching of the doctrine of the Creation should have equal place in the curriculum with the teaching of evolution." Some textbooks have been modified in this sense. "This is absurd. Even religious scientists no longer find it necessary to their position to deny the doctrine of evolution [which] deserves to be called the truth." *Nature* challenged academic scientists working in relevant fields "to affirm that present observations are in their opinion inconsistent with the more commonly accepted views of Earth and species evolution."

Five replies were published.[8] One supported *Nature's* stand; one fully accepted the challenge and denounced the theory of evolution. The other three took a position similar to that maintained in this book, namely that moderate creationist views were not incompatible with a belief in the theory of evolution as a mechanism whereby new species arose from more primitive living forms. But they could not accept the scientific validity of its extrapolation backwards to "zero biological time," so to speak, nor the dogma that the theory sufficed to explain the origin of life on Earth with such certainty that this should be taught as a proven fact. In the light of arguments presented in this book, such caution seems not merely acceptable, but imperative. In his reply Lucas discusses the reasons for the present antipathy toward creationism in all forms, since the ideas were acceptable to the founders of modern science. The current belief that the universe is a closed system that cannot be invaded by the supernatural is not in fact an essential axiom. Scientific principles would be violated only if any supernatural interventions were capricious. Moreover Hume was wrong in arguing that the axiom can be deduced from the success of science.

Summary

Some scientists believe that living organisms arose spontaneously from organic molecules produced abiotically, and that this might happen again—contrary to the principles and experience of bacteriology. Prebiotic organic polymers have the wrong compositions and stereochemical configurations to serve as building blocks for even the most primitive of living organisms. The probability of suitable molecules arising by chance is ludicrously infinitesimal. Scientists who have given serious thought to the problems have been obliged to postulate some guiding principles such as "chemical evolution" and "prescription," which are tantamount to admitting the role of prior intelligence in the creation of living beings.

REFERENCES

[1]S. Fox, *New Scientist*, February 27, 1969, 450.

[2]J.D. Bernal, *The Origin of Life*, Weidenfeld and Nicolson, London, 1967.

[3]J. Oro, S. Nakaparksin, L. Lichtenstein, and E. Gil-Av, *Nature*, 1971, *230*, 105.

[4]C. Ponnamperuma, et al. *Nature*, 1970, *228*, 923.

[5]F.B. Salisbury, *Nature*, 1969, *224*, 342.

[6]B. Butterworth, *Science Group Journal*, Theosophical Research Center, 1970, XIV, No. 4, 115.

[7]Editorial, *Nature*, 1972, *239*, 420.

[8]Garret Vanderhooi, Harold Van Kley, Alan Radcliffe-Smith, E.C. Lucas, *Nature*, 1972, *240*, 365.

Section Three

GENETICS AND EVOLUTION

CHAPTER 9

THE GENETIC CODE

Quite astonishing progress was made during the 1960s in understanding the chemical basis of genetics. This work has already been expounded in popular language many times, but here it is necessary to go into slightly more detail in order to develop the argument. This is, in a nutshell, a campaign against reductionism, i.e. against the prevalent idea that all the phenomena of biological life, including human behavior, can in principle be explained solely in terms of chemistry and physics. Scientists are not, as some people seem to think, cold-blooded calculating machines whose hypotheses never stray one iota beyond what the facts justify. They are as human as other men, and in a flush of enthusiasm over a scientific breakthrough they are apt to let their imagination run away with them. Science writers are even more inclined to do so, often to the point of sensationalism, and they have the more direct influence on popular thought. So, having discovered that some aspects of inheritance can be explained in chemical terms, some of them have fallen into the trap of proclaiming that genetics is *nothing but* chemistry; life itself has been squeezed out of the picture, or has been brashly explained away.

These wonders that have been revealed testify abundantly both to the superhuman ingenuity of the Creative Principle, and to the human ingenuity of the scientists who have puzzled out the mechanisms. But this last is the key word: mechanisms; scientists are not studying Life itself, but the almost unbelievably intricate and delicate tools it uses. This is no criticism either; the study is immensely fascinating and revealing. Modern man has developed an intense curiosity, along with an urge to "explain" everything new in terms of what he already understands. Therefore research into life processes brings great satisfaction, because it promises that life may eventually be neatly and completely described in chemical terms. So it is not really surprising that the materialistic science reporter fails to see the wood for the trees. Another decade of progress at this rate, he prophesies, and it will be possible to create a living creature. Even if the formidable technical difficulties are ignored, it is reasonable to suggest only that some scientist may eventually create a *dead* creature. No more than this is in dispute—just life and death!

The remainder of this chapter attempts to present a balanced account of the triumphs of molecular biology, reserving most of the comments for later chapters.

Genetics and Chromosomes

Everyone knows, in a general way, that the characteristics of any sexual organism are derived from both male and female parent. Also that whereas some of the parental characteristics are expressed, others lie dormant but may reappear in some future generations. The Austrian monk, Mendel, was probably the first to discover the simple laws of inheritance, by his breeding experiments on garden peas. There is no need to explain these laws, and anyhow there are vast complexities that Mendel never dreamed of. What we want to know is *how* these genetic features are passed on; how is all that information inscribed in the tiny germ-cell? Or indeed is it? In the previous Section it is suggested that a nonphysical matrix of intelligence must be postulated to account for the emergence of biological life. However, in evolved modern organisms there is no doubt that a physical structure, the minute cell nucleus, *is* indeed big enough to house a computer with a long memory. This memory is within the nucleus, on the thread-like chromosomes. It is now a familiar story that the germ cells contain only half as many chromosomes as the body cells, so that at union the first cell of the offspring regains the usual complement, half from each parent. When the cell divides (mitosis), each chromosome replicates itself precisely and the new set separates off to form the nucleus of a new cell. This recurs at each division, so that every body cell contains an identical complete set of chromosomes. They come in pairs, similar but not identical; one member of each pair arose originally from the male, the other from the female. So far everything is regular and repetitive. However when the time comes to create new germ cells (meiosis), the behavior is quite different. Instead of replicating, the chromosomes line up in their pairs as if mating, and then instead separate again to form the nuclei of two germ cells. But in separating some go one way, some the other, seemingly by chance, so that although each germ cell contains a complete set of chromosomes, some of them originate from the male, and some from the female. Nor is this the whole story because at the pairing stage the chromosomes seem to become sticky and get tangled up, so that "crossing-over" occurs between corresponding parts of a pair, leading at separation to individual chromosomes of part-male-part-female origin. This shuffling-up can actually be observed under the microscope, and is correlated with the shuffling of parental characteristics that is evident in the offspring. Such observations gave to the science of genetics the possibility of mathematical precision. It gradually became clear that each physical characteristic corresponded with a particular position along the length of a particular chromosome, and fantastically elaborate chromosome maps could eventually be drawn, showing the location of each "gene" that controlled the color of eyes, or whatnot. There is no space for details, but fabulous numbers of breeding experiments on fast-multiplying species were needed. For this purpose the fruit fly *Drosophila* proved very convenient; later, the study of certain microorganisms with sexual stages permitted even more rapid progress. Just one of the principles applied must serve as an illustration. Crossing-over can happen almost anywhere along the length of a chromosome pair. Genes situated near opposite ends of a chromosome will be separated wherever the break occurs, so they behave independently; but genes situated close together will hardly ever separate, and the corresponding characters are said to be "tightly linked," and nearly always occur together in the offspring. The degrees of linkage helped therefore in the construction of chromosome maps. Occasionally some kind of accident occurs in the genetic process and a gene suddenly changes its character in a particular plant or animal, giving rise to a "mutation." These occurrences were noted and utilized by breeders long before their nature was understood.

Chromosome Chemistry

The biologists carried the fascinating story thus far on their own; it becomes well-nigh incredible when the contributions of the biochemists are also brought into the picture.

The chromosomes consist of protein and nucleic acid, but it is the latter which functions as the memory store. To follow the story further it is essential to get an elementary idea of the structures of nucleic acids. They are made up of units called nucleotides. A nucleotide in turn consists of three parts: 1. phosphoric acid; 2. a sugar; 3. a base. The first two can be quickly dismissed, because phosphoric acid is always present, and there are only two sugars: ribonucleic acids (RNA) contain the 5-carbon sugar ribose; deoxyribonucleic acids (DNA) contain deoxyribose with one oxygen less. It is DNA that occurs in the chromosomes. The bases are nitrogenous compounds of two related types, purines and pyrimidines. RNA contains the purines adenine (A) and guanine (G); also the pyrimidines cytosine (C) and uracil (U). DNA also contains the first three, but has thymine (T) instead of uracil. DNA contains long chains of these four nucleotides chemically linked, with hundreds of nucleotide units to each chain. Since they all contain phosphoric acid and deoxyribose, it is only necessary to consider the four bases A, G, C, and T, and the order in which they occur (chemists may refer to Figs. 1 and 2). They hold the key to two remarkable properties of DNA: first, it can replicate itself precisely; second, it carries the genetic code.

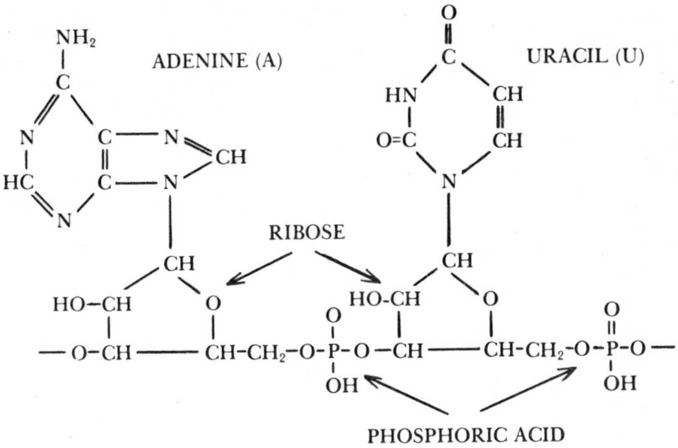

Fig. 1. Part of RNA Chain (2 nucleotides only shown).

PART I

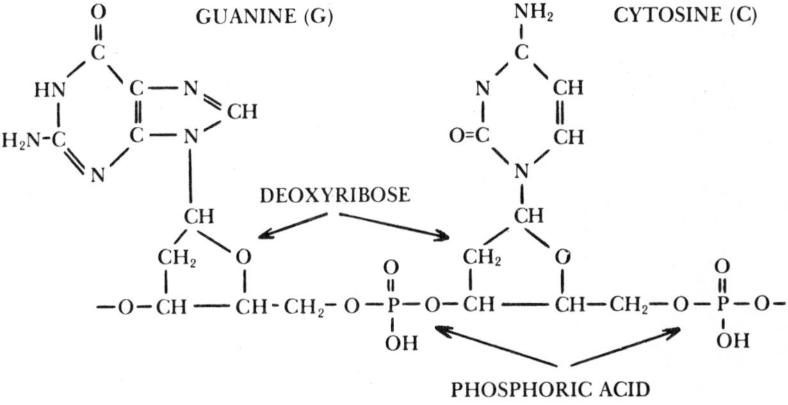

Part of DNA Chain (2 nucleotides only shown (different ones).

PART II

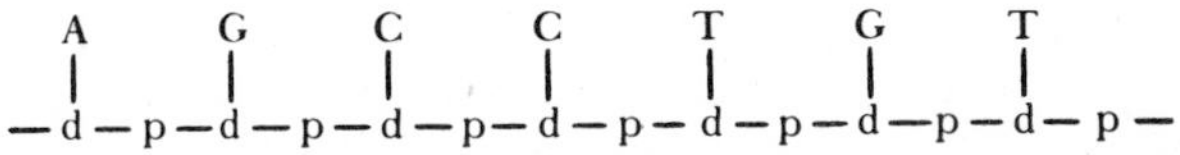

Fig. 2. Simplified diagram of DNA Chain (d=deoxyribose; p=phosphoric acid).

The possibility of replication followed from discoveries about the arrangement of DNA chains in space. A combination of physical measurements were all consistent with a helical shape, or rather with a double helix composed of two DNA strands twisted side by side. The story has been told in a highly readable fashion in Watson's book *The Double Helix*.[1] Watson and Crick in 1953 elaborated this further by showing that the four bases arranged themselves in two complementary pairs. A forms a loose association with T, and G with C (by hydrogen bonding). Opposite to every A in one strand there is a T in the other one, opposite to every G there is a C: and correspondingly of course T mates with A and C with G. In this way the double helix is cross-linked at every base-pair and so acquires cohesion and stability. The whole of one strand is thus complementary to the other: when we know the order of the bases along one we can write down that of its opposite number. (See Fig. 3).

This can now be correlated with what happens when chromosome replication occurs at cell division. Each chromosome is believed to consist essentially of one of these double helices of DNA; the genes are probably just segments of the continuous helices. To replicate, it is supposed that the two strands peel apart from one end, and then each single strand acts as a template for the construction, not of its own likeness, but of its complementary strand. That is to say, every nucleotide in a strand attracts to itself a complementary free nucleotide, A attracting T, C attracting G, and so on. These then link together chemically to make a new strand that winds itself around its template into a new double helix (with one old and one new strand). So when each strand has completely reconstructed its complement, there are two exactly matching double strands ready to pass into the nuclei of the old and the new cell. (See Fig. 4)

At this stage, two highly complex problems presented themselves. The first was to determine the "language" in which the genetic information is written; it is evident that the genetic code is somehow spelled out by the order of the four bases on the DNA strands, but deciphering it was a

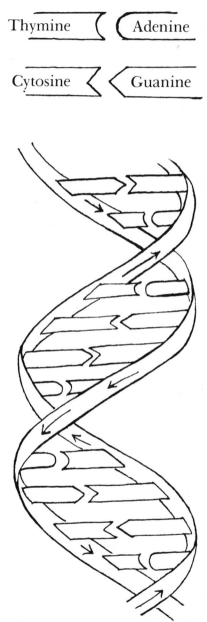

Fig. 3 DNA Double Helix.

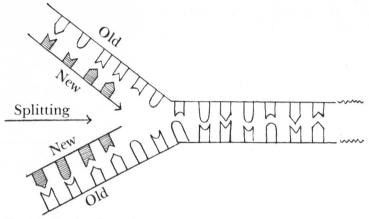

Fig. 4. Replication of complementary strands.

daunting task, which was nevertheless solved within a few years. Secondly, if the code represents a set of instructions, it was necessary to determine by what means they are translated into action within the cell and ultimately within the whole complex organism. It was necessary to solve this second problem in preliminary fashion before the former could be tackled. For the present purpose, however, it is simplest to consider first the elucidation of the genetic code, anticipating only to mention that a gene usually controls the synthesis of a specific enzyme or other protein molecule, so that each "word" codes for one of the amino acids from which the protein is built; also that translation from DNA to protein is not direct but is effected via intermediate transcription of the code onto a molecule of RNA.

The Writing on the Genes

Since the DNA code has only four letters, and the amino acid one has twenty or more, then evidently several bases in their proper sequence must be needed to specify a single amino acid. It is easily calculated that two are not enough, but three are more than enough, because they provide 4 x 4 x 4 = 64 variations. Evidently, therefore, either some combinations do not occur (or if they do, then they convey no message), or else the code is "degenerate," meaning that two or three different combinations spell out the same amino acid.

Various lines of evidence pointed to the fact that each word does in fact comprise a triplet of bases and that they are linked directly together without any signal for a "comma" to divide one triplet from the next. The first steps toward deciphering the code were taken in 1961. When synthetic polyuridine, which carries the code U-U-U—U-U-U— . . ., was added to a suitable cell-free extract from bacteria, it did indeed induce synthesis of protein: this contained the single amino acid phenylalanine, so it appeared that U-U-U was the "code word" for phenylalanine. Other approaches revealed further codewords, but complete elucidation had to wait until synthetic DNA could be made with nucleotides in specified order; by 1967 the complete code was known.

A Universal Language

The words "code" and "cipher" convey perhaps a wrong impression. This genetic code is the antithesis of a military cipher designed to maintain secrecy. Messages in such a code have to be deciphered before they can be understood and finally acted upon. A message in the genetic code, on the contrary, itself initiates direct action. The relation between the nucleic acid bases and amino acids is not arbitrary but inevitable; a particular triplet must itself attract chemically and fit the amino acid it "names" and no other.

The early work on the genetic code was done with bacterial and viral systems. However, later work has fully established the correctness of one's expectation that the code would prove to be universal. Plants and animals use exactly the same language as the microorganisms, which strongly supports the idea of a fundamental unity of life on this planet. It even proved possible to persuade a cell-free bacterial preparation in a test tube to synthesize a rabbit protein under the guidance of rabbit messenger RNA (see later).

The Code in Action

There remained the more complex problem of understanding just how the order of bases on DNA molecules could determine physical characteristics of the living organism, i.e. how instructions are translated into flesh and blood. A vast body of knowledge has been built up, but some of the finer details of this new science of molecular biology have still to be discovered. It is known that many genes operate by controlling the synthesis of particular proteins; specifically these are often enzymes. An enzyme is a protein containing in one region a special molecular arrangement that is able to promote or catalyze some particular chemical reaction. Now it may seem a tall story to suggest that the color of an insect's eye, for example, is controlled by its ability or inability to carry out just one chemical change; nevertheless this could be true, though sometimes several genes are involved jointly. Anyhow, the one-gene-one-enzyme hypothesis can be illusstrated rather dramatically by certain human diseases due to "inborn errors of metabolism." For example, children with phenylketonuria cannot metabolize the amino acid phenylalanine in the normal manner, because the appropriate enzyme is missing. In consequence the phenylalanine is changed only into the corresponding keto-acid; this is excreted in part, but enough remains in the body to damage the brain and cause feeble-mindedness. This, fortunately rare, condition is inherited in exactly the way to be expected if one aberrant gene were involved.

It now seems certain that the order in which the bases are arranged in the DNA chain of a gene controls in some manner the synthesis of a specific protein. Proteins are also long chain-like molecules built up from a collection of unit pieces called amino-acids. These are similar in that they all contain the grouping:

$$H_2N - CH - COOH$$

-NH_2 is the "amino" group (derived from ammonia) and -COOH is the "acid" part. Two amino acids can link head to tail, losing a molecule of water to form a peptide link, thus:

$$H_2N-\overset{\overset{\displaystyle R^1}{|}}{CH}-COOH \; + \; HNH-\overset{\overset{\displaystyle R^2}{|}}{CH}-COOH \longrightarrow$$

$$H_2N-\overset{\overset{\displaystyle R^1}{|}}{CH}-CO-NH-\overset{\overset{\displaystyle R^2}{|}}{CH}-COOH + H_2O$$

This process can be repeated many times over, till 100 or more amino-acids are joined together into a protein molecule:

$$H_2N \overset{\overset{\displaystyle R^1}{|}}{CH} CO-NH \overset{\overset{\displaystyle R^2}{|}}{CH} CO-NH \overset{\overset{\displaystyle R^3}{|}}{CH} CO-NH \overset{\overset{\displaystyle R^4}{|}}{CH} CO-NH \overset{\overset{\displaystyle R^2}{|}}{CH} CO-NH \overset{\overset{\displaystyle R^1}{|}}{CH} CO-$$

The amino acids differ in the nature of the groups R^1, R^2 etc. and there are about twenty of them that occur in ordinary proteins, plus a number of more exotic ones that turn up occasionally. So, rephrasing the problem, it was necessary to find out how a code containing only 4 "letters," A, T, C, G, could spell out instructions for the building of long "words" containing 20 or more letters; and second, how are the instructions carried out? The simplest hypothesis, that the DNA chains might serve *directly* as templates upon which the amino acids would be assembled, is definitely wrong. It is RNA, the second type of nucleic acid, that serves as the actual template or mold for protein building.

Just as the double helix of DNA replicates by untwisting and building up on each of its existing strands a new complementary one, so it is believed that it can serve as a template upon which RNA strands (the working molds) can be built up, again with a complementary order of bases to maintain the code. This type of RNA has been imaginatively christened messenger RNA. Thus the gene DNA is the master template, the messenger RNA the secondary or acting template. It is the latter that transports the message to the protein assembly units; there, with the help of another type of RNA called soluble or transfer RNA, the amino acids are brought up in turn, as the code instructs, and linked into a protein chain. The protein assembly units are called ribosomes; these are minute complex organized bodies within the cell (described in more detail later). Along with mitochondria and other complex particles, they are known collectively as organelles.

The Central Dogma

The end of this phase of molecular biology was signalled by Crick's bold hypothesis triumphantly named the central dogma. It is very simply expressed in the little diagram below, which proclaims that genetic information in DNA is always transferred to RNA before being expressed in protein, and that both steps are irreversible; protein cannot exert any influence on RNA or DNA, nor RNA on DNA. However, as Chapter 10 will explain, this central dogma is now discredited, at least in part.

$$DNA \longrightarrow RNA \longrightarrow protein$$

Later Refinements

The current stage in molecular biology comprises revision, elaboration and refinement of the earlier hypotheses, which were recognized as being oversimplified. For example, the mode of replication of the DNA double helix is by no means so straightforward as was originally supposed. It now appears (1972) that the effective enzyme may at last have been discovered, but the work still has to be confirmed.

Most of the research in this field has been done with bacteria, and there have been doubts whether all the conclusions are applicable to other species. For example, in bacteria the chromosomes are loose and not enclosed in a nucleus as in higher organisms. Thus there is no barrier to the necessary physical contact between the coded DNA and the growing strand of messenger RNA, nor subsequently between this and the ribosomes where protein is made, whereas in higher organisms the wall of the nucleus presents difficulties.

To illustrate the growing complexity, it may be recalled that at least six distinct types of nucleic acid have been revealed. There is the fundamental chromosomal DNA of as many kinds as there are genes. RNAs with so far incompletely specified function are present in the nucleus, and two more kinds in the ribosomes. Then there is coded messenger RNA, again of as many kinds as there are genes, and finally transfer RNA, seemingly one kind for each amino acid.

Ribosomes

Perhaps the most fascinating cellular organelles are the ribosomes. Their size is known, and the fact that they readily dissociate into a large and a small subunit; the larger unit is known to contain a single long strand of RNA and about 60 different proteins, while the smaller also has a single strand of RNA and about 20 different proteins. It has not been possible to determine their structure experimentally because they are too small to reveal much detail to the electron microscope and they have not yet been crystallized, so X-ray crystallography cannot be applied. These difficulties have, however, not deterred R. A. Cox of the National Institute for Medical Research, London, from trying to build models that could account for their behavior. In this he has been uncannily successful, his imagination having doubtless been stimulated by ten years' research on ribosomal RNA. Various lines of evidence led him to formulate the RNA of the larger unit as a single-stranded molecule with about one hundred loops of different sizes and compositions; at the base of each loop the RNA is supposed to be folded back on itself to make what is in effect a double-stranded segment that coils into a small helix. The smaller unit similarly has around fifty loops in its RNA. Since there are about half as many protein molecules as loops, a pair is supposed to be associated with each globular protein molecule. Using wire for the RNA, wound round short stout rods in the helical segments, and plastic balls for the protein molecules, Cox built up models for the strands of ribonuclear protein. By folding these back and forth into sheets he was able to construct a plausible ribosome model of the correct dimensions. For the larger unit the sheet is bent into a horseshoe shape and the smaller one fits over its opening like a cap. This model accords with all the known facts. Among other features it provides a groove between the subunits into which messenger RNA can fit, and a hole from which the growing protein chain can emerge. The model is unlikely to be completely accurate but its great value is that it suggests many predictions that can be tested and so it provides stimulus for fruitful research.

The ribosome model has been described in some detail for several reasons: it is fascinating in its own right; it is a splendid example of the working of the inspired imagination (see Section I, Chapter 6), and it illustrates the fantastic ordered complexity of a cellular organelle. A fast-growing bacterium may contain some 15,000 of these ribosomes, each of which can produce a complete protein molecule in about ten seconds. Moreover, ribosomes are only one type of organelle; there are also, for example, the important and semiautonomous mitochondria, which carry a battery of membrane-bound enzymes. It has been suggested that they may be derived from formerly independent microorganisms that have become captured and condemned to symbiotic existence within another organism. Plants carry their chlorophyll, the green pigment that enables them to use the energy of sunlight for chemical synthesis, in organelles of another elaborately structured type, called chloroplasts; these too may have been derived from originally free-living organisms; in this instance algae.

It is clear that living things are structured with extreme precision at every order of magnitude. With the naked eye we can perceive, for example, the architecture of the feathers on a bird's wings, and may appreciate the elaborately coordinated arrangement of muscles and nerves that move them in precisely controlled flight. Under the microscope we can see a similar system, scaled down perhaps a hundred-fold, to serve the needs of a barely visible gnat. The microscope also reveals highly regular dispositions of cells of various types within both plants and animals. The cells in turn are not filled with amorphous "protoplasm" but contain numerous organized structures such as the organelles mentioned above, revealed by the electron microscope. Finally molecular biology shows that the nucleic acids, proteins, carbohydrates, fats, etc., in these cells are composed of precisely ordered sequences of their respective chemical subunits; every molecule of the enzyme pepsin, for instance, contains exactly the same amino acids in the same order. All these facts give point to the contention that human ingenuity is unlikely to succeed in reconstructing a complete living organism; *furthermore it is even less likely that one could ever have evolved by itself without intelligent guidance.*

Integration of Cell Function

The most unsatisfactory feature of molecular biology so far has been its piecemeal character. There is some understanding about how various bits of the mechanism work, but none about the entity as a whole. Yet clearly the unicellular organism does function as a dimly conscious entity, integrating all the mechanisms to serve its overall purpose. Each cell in a higher plant or animal has a similar measure of autonomy and should also be accorded some measure of consciousness, but here it serves the overriding purpose of the limb, organ, or gland of which it forms a part, and these in turn are integrated by the bodily consciousness of the creature as a whole. Latterly there have been attempts to view molecular biology from these wider angles. The key problem is control and how it is exercised. Every cell in an animal body carries in its nucleus the organism's entire informational complement of genes, but at any time only a few of them are functional. If they all operated, then disorganized undifferentiated growth would occur—and the name for this is cancer. So it has been clear for some time that besides operator genes there must be either activator genes that switch them on, or regulator genes that turn them off; these in turn must somehow be sensitive to commands from the organism, or must respond automatically when the concentration of any particular enzyme becomes too low or too high. Jacob and Monod favored the idea of regulator genes, which were supposed to send out repressor molecules to turn off operator genes. Harris favored a positive control mechanism with activators. Support has been forthcoming for both hypotheses, but it now looks as though they may both become absorbed into a more elaborate one proposed by R.J. Britten and E.H. Davidson of the Carnegie Institute, Washington. They start from the observation that the amount of DNA per cell increases steeply along the evolutionary scale. Thus a mammal may have ten times as much as a fish and one thousand times as much as a bacterium, yet the number of biochemical functions to be controlled by the genes does not increase to anything like the same extent. Thus the higher organisms have a great many "surplus" genes, which are available for regulatory purposes; it is reasonable to suppose that evolutionary progress is indeed marked by increasing precision of biochemical control. This hypothesis is too complex to describe here in detail, but it involves coordinated interaction of producer, receptor, sensor, and integrator genes operating via activator RNA molecules. This work represents a welcome approach to a holistic or systems approach to the intricate mechanisms of biological life.

However, all these achievements in elucidating mechanisms have created the impression that they represent the whole story, that "it's all in the genetic code," and that genetic information does not merely perpetuate itself in an apparently automatic fashion, but even somehow created itself in the same way.

Actually it strains credulity far less to postulate an intelligent guiding principle than to imagine all this intricately ordered complexity arising of its own accord.

Summary

The science of genetics has been reduced to molecular terms by the discovery of the genetic code. Chromosomes comprise mainly very long double helices of deoxyribonucleic acid (DNA), of which the genes are sections. Genetic information is inscribed thereon as sequences of triplets of the four nucleotides present in DNA: each prescribes a specific amino acid, and the whole gene prescribes a specific enzyme or other protein. The DNA helix can replicate itself and can transcribe its genetic information onto ribonucleic acid (RNA) which is the intermediary in guiding protein synthesis: this takes place on highly organized cellular structures called ribosomes. Only a proportion of the genes present are functional at any moment in any cell and elaborate control mechanisms have been postulated.

It is emphasized that all this elaboration could not conceivably have arisen without intelligent guidance and that molecular biology describes a mechanism and does not reveal the secret of life, as has sometimes been suggested.

It has become clear that the genes represent the repertoire of the cell: at any instant only a proportion of them are actively performing, while the rest lie dormant until called into action by a need, which may be local at the cellular level, or may be dictated by an organ or by the body as a whole. It is not widely recognized that revelation of this hierarchy of intricate interlocking control systems does not resolve the ultimate mystery, but on the contrary deepens it. The more complex the mechanisms are shown to be, the more need there is to postulate intelligent programming.

REFERENCE

[1]Watson, *The Double Helix*, Wedenfeld and Nicolson, London, 1968.

CHAPTER 10

DOUBTS AND RESERVATIONS

Most molecular biologists have been exultant about the phenomenal progress in their field of research, and have openly said they were getting close to the secret of life. Others, however, have felt revulsion at these rashly mechanistic hypotheses. Molecular biologists have elevated their theories almost to the status of religious doctrine, even including a "central dogma." Vast numbers of new research programs have been formulated on the basis of these theories, and the results will inevitably tend to reinforce them. They are now so firmly entrenched that opposition tends to be brushed aside as tiresome heresy. Nevertheless there has been criticism, not only by biologists such as Barry Commoner, but also by experienced elder scientists like Sir Cyril Hinshelwood, a Past President of the Royal Society.

This chapter is necessarily rather technical; readers who do not want to bother with theories of molecular biology can turn directly to the conclusions at the end of the chapter.

Cytoplasmic Factors in Inheritance

Objections to the orthodox Watson-Crick theories are actually of two types, though they may overlap. The first, as exemplified by Commoner, denies the *inviolability* of the coded sequence on DNA and suggests that it, and the events it determines, may be altered by external circumstances, or by internal feedback from the later steps in the chain of events. The second denies instead the *exclusiveness* of nuclear DNA in controlling inheritance; it provides evidence for additional "extrachromosomal" hereditary factors, i.e. controls situated in the cytoplasm of the cell besides those residing in the nucleus. In addition to the work in microbial systems by Sir Cyril Hinshelwood and others, there is some direct evidence that inheritance is not determined solely by chromosomal DNA in higher animals.

One of the consequences of the Mendelian rules of inheritance is that continuous close interbreeding should so redistribute the genes that individuals eventually approach uniformity in genetic constitution. Plant breeders use this principle to get pure lines of vegetables and flowering plants that come true from seed; they do, up to a point, but subtle differences in color shades, size, vigor, and form persist, even when the plants are grown under identical cultural conditions, insofar as this is possible. Animal breeders, too, work in the same manner to maintain the breeds of dogs, for instance. But dog-lovers would indignantly refute any suggestion that dogs of a breed are nearly identical, and dog shows would not be possible if they were. Suppliers of laboratory rats and mice have used even more intensive inbreeding (brother-sister mating) to achieve uniformity. But their "standard" animals still show disconcerting individuality in their responses to drugs and experimental diets. Professor Roger Williams of the University of Texas has studied these variations instead of shrugging them off as an annoyance. He has demonstrated large differences in urine composition among such animals on the same diet, and differences up to sixty-fold in their voluntary selection of foodstuffs, the amount of exercise they take, and so forth.

These observations point to some factors in inheritance, besides the genes, that control differentiation of the embryo into the cells of different types that form the various organs. It would appear that this differentiation, which occurs in all higher organisms, does introduce a new feature, and that the full story of the chemistry of inheritance cannot be learned by study of unicellular organisms that do not differentiate. Direct proof was hard to obtain until Williams recalled the reproductive peculiarities of the nine-banded armadillo. In this animal only a single egg cell is fertilized, but it invariably divides to yield four embryos, in which the genes must be identical, and the animal always gives birth to identical quadruplets. Despite their genetic identity, in terms of inheritance determined by nuclear DNA, armadillo quadruplets still differed considerably from one another in organ weights and biochemical features. In all, twenty parameters were measured in sixteen sets of quadruplets, and differences up to 140-fold were found within a set. At the two successive divisions that separate the four embryos, the four nuclei are replicated identically, but it is concluded that the other complex organelles in the cytoplasm are not equally divided, and that these must carry additional inheritance factors that account for the observed variations among the quadruplets.

Central Dogma Discredited

Reverting to the assumed inviolability of the coded information on chromosomal DNA, the blunt comment made by Barry Commoner in one of his papers in Nature may first be quoted;[1] he expressed himself in the terse phrases:

> DNA is *not* a self-duplicating molecule.
> DNA is *not* the master chemical of the cell.
> DNA is *not* the secret of life, but instead,
> Life is the secret of DNA.

The first statement may need elaboration; for replication, DNA needs not only a supply of the four nucleotides but the help of at least one enzyme and possibly some initiator substance to start the process. In other words it does not occur automatically as the term self-duplicating seems to imply.

The central dogma is expressed in the formula:

$$DNA \longrightarrow RNA \longrightarrow protein$$

This dogma is one of the overconfident predictions that have in part at least been discredited. The various gene-regulating mechanisms represent a feedback effect of the product upon the original producing system, namely DNA. A more serious fault of the dogma is that the first arrow can sometimes be reversed, as recent work has shown beyond doubt, so that RNA carrying information in the genetic code can serve as a template upon which correspondingly coded DNA can be formed. The first indication was given by H. Temin who, as far back as 1964, believed that the induction of cancer in animals by RNA viruses provided evidence that their RNA could modify the coding of the host DNA. He claimed to have found a stretch of DNA that matched the nucleotide sequence on the RNA of the virus infecting the cells. If true this would contravene the central dogma, but Temin's evidence was circumstantial and was not generally accepted. Recently, however, with S. Mizutasi,[2] he has published additional work of a more direct character, suggesting that his original conclusions were right. Almost simultaneously and independently his results, implying violation of the central dogma, were confirmed in two other laboratories. Spiegelman, for example, reported finding in six different tumor-inducing RNA viruses an enzyme that could synthesize DNA on RNA templates. Further confirmatory papers appeared promptly and the reality of the reverse transcriptase enzyme, as it was soon called, became firmly established.

During 1971 and 1972 high levels of reverse transcriptase were found in white blood cells from leukemia patients and in malignant tumor tissues, but not in corresponding normal cells.[3]

Crick had promptly leaped to the defense of his dogma, claiming that it was never intended to exclude the possibility that RNA might in exceptional circumstances code for DNA. But almost everyone else thought both arrows in the diagram were meant to be irrevocably one-way, and no attempt was made to dispel this general misunderstanding, if such it was, until Temin's work was confirmed.

It seems clear that the Watson-Crick theories are correct in essence, though they are now seen to be wrong in their excessive rigidity and in the central dogma of irreversibility. Even the conclusions drawn from the highly technical researches involved are difficult to express simply, but they seem important enough to justify the attempt with the help of diagrams adapted from one of Commoner's papers.[4] Fig. 5 sets out the orthodox Watson-Crick theory in some detail. Translation of the code into specific protein is now recognized to be quite a complex procedure, but it is claimed that the whole sequence stems inexorably and solely from self-duplicating DNA as determinant. As outlined in Chapter 9, the code is first retranscribed as a sequence of nucleotides onto messenger ribonucleic acid. This is what actually specifies the sequence of amino acids to be built into the protein molecule. The assembly operation is performed on a kind of jig called a ribosome (see Chapter 9), but first the amino acids have to be linked in turn to nucleic acid molecules of a third sort, called transfer ribonucleic acid, and at least two enzymes are needed as workmen on the assembly line. However, none of these agents is supposed to have any influence on the pattern of inheritance, and so their auxiliary role is indicated by a single arrow; double arrows indicating a determinant role proceed only from DNA through messenger-RNA and protein, and so on to the inherited metabolic pathway that it controls. The pattern can be changed only by a mutation, which chemically alters one or more of the DNA nucleotides, and so changes the code at these points.

In complete contrast, Commoner's views are illustrated in Fig. 6, where almost every agent is accorded a double arrow signifying that it has some influence on the hereditary pattern; each alteration from Fig. 5 is justified by citation of work published mostly from laboratories other than his own. By introducing feedback at numerous points, this scheme denies the central dogma of irreversibility. Commoner also believes that the polymerase enzyme may sometimes influence the sequence of replicating DNA, i.e. it has more than a passively catalytic role; accordingly he replaces the unique triple arrow with a double one. Commoner's ideas, including these latest ones, have been strongly criticized on the grounds that he has misinterpreted some of the evidence. Only other molecular biol-

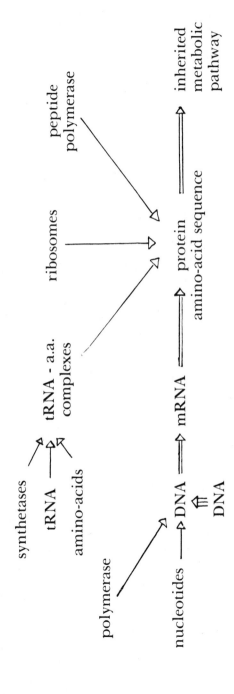

Fig. 5. Representation of the Watson-Crick theory. A single arrow signifies that an agent is necessary for the formation of the product but does not contribute to the biochemical specificity of that product. A double arrow signifies that an agent does contribute to the specificity of the product. A triple arrow signifies that specificity is derived solely from an identical preceding molecule, capable therefore of self-duplication. (a.a.=amino acid.)

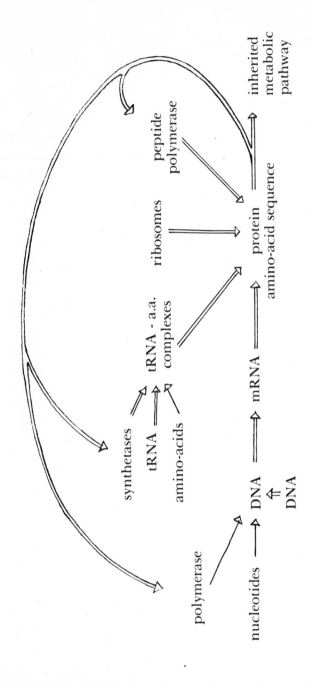

Fig. 6. In contrast to the Watson–Crick theory, this diagram suggests that the biochemical specificity of inheritance is of multimolecular origin rather than originating in DNA alone and that the transfer system is circular rather than linear.

ogists are really qualified to judge the issue, and most of them lean heavily toward the orthodox theories.

Without implying support for every detail of Commoner's hypothesis, it might fairly be said that Fig. 5 illustrates the sort of tidy one-way world a chemist would dream up, whereas Fig. 6 looks more like that of a real biologist. It includes the circular chicken-and-egg dilemma (which came first?) that we find throughout the real world of nature. Surely the ultimate determinant is life itself, not a chemical substance, not even one so remarkable as DNA. As Weiss puts it,[5] "life is process and not substance"—so the secret of life cannot reside in DNA. Fig. 5 represents a straightjacket that confines life, Fig. 6 a versatile mechanism that life can manipulate for its purposes. The final paragraph of Commoner's paper makes an appropriate conclusion:

> Biologists have confronted successively—like a nest of Chinese boxes—levels of complexity ranging from the ecosystem to the internal chemistry of the cell. The last box has now been opened. According to the Watson-Crick theory, it should have contained the single source of all the inherited specificity of living organisms—DNA. It is my view that we now know that the last box is empty and that the inherited specificity of life is derived from nothing less than life itself.

Men or Molecules

Most of the work in molecular biology is done in test tubes, with highly artificial systems, using cell preparations mainly from mutated microorganisms and viruses that often do not even exist in the natural state. Moreover the interferences with heredity that are alleged to occur represent the effects of foreign enzymes. ribosomes, etc., from a different species, a situation that does not normally arise with healthy whole organisms. Thus the precise relevance to higher animals and man of all this academic work in molecular biology is still problematical.

The Nobel Laureate, Sir Macfarlane Burnet, writing in 1966 for the "Dogma Disputed" series in the *Lancet*, subtitled his paper "A Tilt at Molecular Biology."[6] He criticizes it not for its errors but rather for its self-indulgence and irrelevance to the rest of biology and medicine. It has created the belief that "there is nothing substantial in biological research apart from working out the implications of the sequence of nucleotides in DNA." Thus manpower and funds are diverted from lines of research that he, as a medical man, would consider more valuable. "The first quarrel that a physician and a biologist will have with molecular biology as now practiced is that the subject is very largely a laboratory artefact that has never been brought into useful relation with biological realities." He complains that most of the work has been done with "rough" strains of bacteria that have become altered from their natural state in laboratory culture, and with viruses (bacteriophages) that have no function other than to prey on these bacteria—a remote and academic corner of biology.

> There is a disconcerting analogy between the progress of atomic physics and of molecular biology. . . . We have been able to construct a model of what happens in the stars and find no use for it except self-destruction. . . . The human implications of what is going on in this sophisticated universe of tissue-cultured cells, bacteria, and the viruses which can be grown at the expense of one or other are at best dubious, at worst frankly terrifying.

It has been optimistically suggested that eventually genetic engineering may be able to correct some rare inborn errors of metabolism, and eventually perhaps to improve upon an individual's genetic make-up. Meanwhile Burnet believes that a deadly hazard in this work is not being taken seriously enough; the deliberate creation of viral mutants could conceivably start a world-wide disaster if a particularly lethal one were accidently released. In fairness it should be added that since these criticisms were written, a number of molecular biologists have applied their techniques to mammalian structures.

Conclusions

Most of the conclusions of this chapter can be given in the words of Ludwig von Bertalanffy, in quotations from his contribution to the 1968 Alpbach Symposium "Beyond Reductionism."[7]

The ultimate "reduction" of the phenomena of life to the molecular properties of DNA and related substances as promised in popular accounts of molecular biology, appears somewhat less than convincing. If anything, organisms are organized things, with regard to both structure and function, exhibiting hierarchical order, differentiation, interaction of innumerable processes, goal-directed behavior, negentropic trends, and related criteria. About these, the mechanistic approach—not excluding molecular biology—is silent. The reason is not simply imperfect knowledge, so that the discovery of some new enzyme, or a new electromicroscopic structure would close the gap. The trouble is rather that the conventional categories, concepts and models of physics and chemistry do not deal with the organismic aspect that I have mentioned. They seem to leave out just what is specific to living things and life processes.

The organismic conception has definite implications with respect to the genetic code . . . . The code, obviously, cannot be a fortuitous string of "words" (nucleotide triplets) comparable to the "word salad" produced by a schizophrenic. In some way, there must be organization—otherwise the DNA code would produce, at best, a heap of proteins, not an organized system, a bacterium, fly or human being. We presently know the *vocabulary* of the code, the triplets standing for amino acids; but we do not know its *grammar,* the meaning of the message as a whole. This "grammar" (or programme, or algorithm for producing an organism, contrasted to bits of information provided by individual codons) is unknown, but must be postulated.

To put it more briefly, the secret of life is surely that life was there all the time, though in its primordial state it is more aptly named "order" or "intelligence." When conditions on the earth were suitable, life "emerged" in the form of primitive biological organisms, but it was not created *de novo* out of chemical substances.

Summary

The rigid Watson-Crick theories on molecular genetics

have been challenged. Chromosomal DNA is not in exclusive control of inheritance: there is good evidence for additional controlling factors outside the nucleus. The "central dogma" proclaiming that information flows in one direction only, from DNA via RNA to specific proteins, has been definitely overthrown in respect of the first step, and other feedback effects have been postulated. The phenomena of life cannot be fully explained in terms of nucleic acid chemistry; "life" in the guise of order or intelligence must surely predate biological life.

REFERENCES

[1]Barry Commoner, *Nature,* 1964, *202,* 960.
[2]H. Temin and S. Mizutasi, *Nature,* 1970, *226,* 1211.
[3]S. Spiegelman and R. Gallo, *Nature New Biology,* 1972, *240,* 67, 72.
[4]Barry Commoner, *Nature,* 1969, *220,* 334.
[5]Arthur Koestler and J.R. Smythies, *Beyond Reductionism,* Hutchinson, London, 1969. Contribution to Symposium discussion by Paul Weiss.
[6]F.M. Burnet, *Lancet,* 1966, *1,* 37.
[7]Ludwig von Bertalanffy, Ref. 5, p. 58.

CHAPTER 11

INTERFERING WITH HEREDITY

Having uncovered this wealth of knowledge about genetics, it is natural that biologists wish to put it to practical use. This chapter reviews briefly some of their accomplishments and also their hopes for the future. The latter must be taken seriously, for although the ideas are speculative, they are in the same class as speculations in the early 1940s as to whether an atom bomb could be made, and in the 1950s as to whether men would walk on the moon. The will and the money are available, and the remaining problems are likely to be solved.

The words "interfering with heredity" or "genetic engineering" tend to conjure up macabre images of unnatural and unholy practices. But in fact we have been unconcernedly influencing the heredity of plants and animals for centuries. What does bother us is the possibility that new techniques may be invented that are applicable to man. Whenever we pollinate a flower or mate dogs we provide an opportunity for recombinations of genes that might never occur in nature. When we nurture the best of the progeny for further breeding and cull the rest, we are applying *un*-natural selection; we choose, not as nature does, for survival value, but for some characteristics that give us aesthetic pleasure or economic advantage.

In some plant breeding stations such work is done with extreme precision and sophistication, even to the extent of introducing into a cereal a single specified gene from another strain or species. New strains of wheat and rice so produced give higher yields, respond better to fertilizers, or contain more protein or protein of better nutritional value, or embody resistance to fungal diseases—or indeed combine several of these advantages. They have enabled some of the poorer countries to overcome undernutrition and even to become exporters of cereal instead of importers.

Genetic Engineering

Such achievements well deserve the description "genetic engineering," but in fact the term is usually restricted to direct manipulation of chromosomes, which can be done in either of two ways. The first is to induce a mutation, which is an actual change in a gene, altering its coded message through chemical change in a segment of its DNA. This can be done by bombardment with neutrons or electrons (β rays) or by γ-, X- or ultra-violet radiation, or by one of many known mutagenic chemicals. This approach is rather like firing at a target with a blunderbuss at maximum range while blindfolded; the score of bullseyes would be negligibly small. The analogy of the blunderbuss is apt because radiation provides numerous projectiles only approximately pointed toward the extremely small target. The blindfold illustrates that we do not really know where the target is within the gene, nor exactly what we need to do to it, in order to produce a desirable mutation. In practice, well over ninety-nine percent of mutations are deleterious if not actually lethal. This may still not matter if, for example, we are trying to breed a crop plant for resistance to a pathogenic fungus. Many thousands of seeds are irradiated, then germinated, and the small seedlings are sprayed liberally with spores of the fungus. It kills almost all of them, but we are interested only in the few mutated resistant ones that survive. Undesirable traits may also have been introduced, but they can be bred out in a few generations, to produce a strain with all the original features plus resistance to the fungus.

Second, and more selectively, ways can be sought to introduce into the cell nucleus specific genetic material that the host organism will accept and use as its own. Ordinary breeding programs allow manipulation of the normal processes of sexual reproduction for our own purposes. But both these other forms of genetic engineering also follow nature's methods; mutations occur spontaneously, probably caused by radiation, one of the agents we employ deliberately; introduction of new genetic material is precisely the procedure of viruses and bacterial transforming factors.

Heritance of Acquired Characteristics

The long controversy may be recalled between the Lamarckians, who championed the idea of the inheritability of acquired characteristics, and the geneticists, who held that nothing could be transmitted to the next generation that was not already present in the germ cells of the parents. See also Chapter 12. In Russia, the former theory was upheld by Lysenko, who was in turn supported and encouraged by the regime, because these ideas fitted in better with communist principles. In the West, on the other hand, Lysenkoism was reviled as a dreadful example of the prostitution of science by the state—akin to the new race theories promulgated by scientists in Nazi Germany, and elsewhere even now.

It was therefore surprising to see a paper with the title "Heritance of Acquired Characters" by F.L. Horsefall, who was president and director of the Sloane-Kettering Institute for Cancer Research in New York.[1] This paper did not herald some startling new discovery, but was in the nature of a new look at some earlier work on "transformation" in baceria, which was indeed startling enough in its time. It has not usually been interpreted in this fashion because it does not really conflict with orthodox genetical theories, but can now be considered as a natural extension of them. So this paper provides an interesting example of how two irreconcilable scientific theories may sometimes be bridged. Nevertheless it affords no support whatever for the Lamarckian explanations given by Lysenko for his plant-breeding results.

The work in question upon pneumococci, the organisms that cause pneumonia, was reported nearly twenty years previously by Avery, Macleod, and McCarty. More specifically it involved experiments with two related strains of pneumococci, one virulent, the other harmless. DNA was extracted from the virulent strain and added to cultures of the other. These then acquired the virulent properties of the first strain, and moreover remained virulent on repeated subculture, i.e. the new property was propagated indefinitely. This was the first demonstration that pure nucleic acid could have biological activity, and in a sense it paved the way for the modern concept that DNA is the matrix upon which is written the genetic code of the genes. This "transformation" of the bacteria involves addition of completely new genetic material which is incorporated and adopted as its own by the organism.

The added DNA is not itself the virulent agent; what it does is to direct the biosynthesis of a new polysaccharide in the outer capsule of the bacterium, and this is what makes the organism virulent. Horsefall goes on to point out that some viruses can behave in an exactly similar manner. Viruses also consist largely of nucleic acid bearing genetic information, yet several of them have been obtained in beautiful crystals, suggesting that in themselves they are just "dead" molecules, despite their terrifying potentialities. Detailed studies of a bacteriophage (a virus that attacks a bacterium) by electron microscopy, among other means, have revealed the details of the attack. The phage particle attaches itself to the bacterium, then by a mechanism akin to a hypodermic syringe, injects its DNA. This then takes over, displacing the normal metabolism of the bacterium and forcing it instead to relinquish its substance for the creation of many new phage particles; the bacterium finally bursts and the phage is released to attack other bacteria. Most of the viruses that prey on bacteria eventually kill their hosts, having first enslaved them to produce more virus material. However, this does not always happen; one such example is the harmless (non-toxigenic) strain of diphtheria baccillus. When invaded by appropriate viruses, these organisms produce, under the direction of the viral DNA, a highly toxic protein—diphtheria toxin. In this instance, the union between baccillus and virus can be permanent; the baccillus suffers no premature death but goes on multiplying in its new toxigenic form. Virus cannot normally be isolated from these organisms, except that under exceptional conditions of growth, dissociation can occur and virus can then be recovered. In other words, as with the "transforming principle," the new genetic information is integrated with the cell's own genes, and the two go on working together in a kind of intimate symbiotic union.

It is obviously more difficult to achieve any such kind of transformation in multicelled higher organisms. In the first instance, there is little prospect of injected DNA passing through several membranes and getting to the nucleus before it is degraded. Then it would have to be accepted and become integrated with the cell's own chromosomes, so that it was replicated during cell division and passed on via the germ cells to the next generation. Also, in order to exercise any function, it would need to be transcribed onto messenger RNA to direct the synthesis of protein. Claims to have converted one variety of duck into another by injecting DNA from the latter type have been disputed and not confirmed. However, some success for this simple technique seems to have been achieved in plants, simply by adding bacterial DNA to barley seedlings. The work still requires confirmation in another laboratory but L. Ledoux and R. Huart in Belgium have already provided impressive evidence for incorporation of bacterial DNA into the barley plants, where it directs the synthesis of new protein, and also for transmission of the genetic information to the seed.[2]

However, to induce useful changes in higher organisms, it would be necessary to introduce natural or synthetic genes coding for known and useful proteins, and until recently the prospect seemed remote. Recent work, however, has demonstrated the possibility of modifying existing genes (or viruses) by chemically adding nucleotide sequences. Further, in 1970, Khorana succeeded with the total synthesis of a small gene from yeast containing seventy-seven pairs of nucleotides. Fifteen short lengths of single-stranded DNA were first synthesized by purely chemical means; they were linked together in the correct order, with the help of an enzyme, to construct in stepwise fashion the two complementary strands of double-stranded DNA that make up the gene. A similar elaborate technique might eventually be used to synthesize new genes that do not exist in nature.

Genetic Transfer from Virus to Man

The tranquilizing thought that there was no likelihood of finding ways to transfer such foreign genes, whether natural or synthetic, into man has also received a rude shock recently; it has already happened, by accident! It was indeed already known that infective viruses operate by transferring their genetic information into the host cells. But this is a temporary happening, for the pathogenic viruses kill the cells they infect, so the viral information is eliminated from the host when the disease subsides. However, like some bacterial transforming factors (as noted earlier) some viruses can become passengers, infecting a host but doing no detectable damage, even though they may cause disease in other species. Such a virus is the Shope Papilloma virus that induces warts, but only in rabbits and also only if it comes into contact with abraded skin. In other species that show no sign of disease on introduction of the virus the viral information could either be lost or latent, or it could become a more or less permanent operational part of the animal's genetic information. As it happens there is a simple test, for the Shope virus is known to carry in its DNA the nucleotide sequence that is the code for synthesis of arginase, an enzyme that degrades arginine, one of the common amino acids of food proteins. Correspondingly it was found that rabbits, rats and mice infected with the virus do show abnormally low levels of arginine in their blood, showing that it contains the arginine-destroying enzyme arginase; the abnormal presence of this enzyme suggests in turn that it is synthesized by the animals in response to "instructions" introduced by the virus.

It occurred to Stanfield Rogers of the Oak Ridge

National Laboratory, Tennessee, that it would be interesting to test people known to have worked with the Shope virus in laboratories.[3] Sure enough, about half of them did have blood arginine levels well below the lower limit of normal levels, showing that they had become accidentally infected and that at least this item of the viral information had indeed been integrated into their chromosomes and had remained operational. Fortunately it did them no harm. On the contrary, there are a few rare individuals for whom such viral infection might do some good. Two cases of arginaemia have been described: these individuals evidently lack the normal means of metabolizing the amino acid arginine and carry high concentrations of it in their blood; this results in mental retardation and other abnormalities. Such cases, if diagnosed early enough, might conceivably be cured by infection with the Shope virus to enable them to synthesize the enzyme needed to destroy their excess of arginine.

The future for human genetic engineering is believed to lie with transduction of semisynthetic viruses; that is to say, viruses will be used to transport new genetic information, including chemically synthesized genes, into the human cell nucleus. Moreover, these possibilities no longer lie in the realms of science fiction; they could well happen in the 1980s if not sooner. Already it has proved possible, for example, to add to tobacco mosaic virus sequences of polyadenylic acid, i.e. a length of synthetic RNA carrying the code — A — A — A — which induces synthesis of the peptide polylysine. This modified virus duly infected the tobacco leaves and induced synthesis of polylysine; the new virus replicated in the plant and could be recovered unchanged from the leaves. This could even be useful if it would work in some food plant, to make it more nutritious by increasing the proportion of lysine in its protein, lysine being an essential amino acid in which plant proteins tend to be deficient. This, however, is only preliminary research. Natural sequences of nucleotides can be isolated as messenger RNA, and unnatural ones will be synthesized, for linking with the RNA of harmless viruses, which hopefully can then transfer these genes into the nucleus of animal or human cells. As Stanfield Rogers comments:

> Clearly, science now has the basic capabilities to use viruses as vectors to transmit operational genetic information. In the future such techniques will have profound effects upon the effective treatment of many different diseases, to say nothing of the possibilities of increasing the nutritional value of foods at a time when this may be critical to the survival of mankind.

If this does come about, it seems likely that the initial revulsion against such techniques will soon be overcome, and that we shall become reconciled to them as we are now to other bizarre methods such as leucotomy and electric shock treatment for mental disorders.

Parthenogenic Reproduction

Gardeners are familiar with vegetative propagation as a means of perpetuating plant varieties. For example it is done with chrysanthemums by cuttings, or with roses by budding. Recently discussed has been the startling possibility of doing something similar with animals or men—a notion that evoked the newspaper headline "New Einsteins from Cuttings." Germ cells contain only half as many chromosomes as body cells; the full complement is restored at fertilization by combination of the chromosomes from the two parents, so that each contributes to the genetic make-up of the offspring. But if the nucleus from a body cell already containing the full number of chromosomes could be introduced into an ovum from which its own nucleus had been removed, and if this could then be successfully implanted into a womb and brought to term, the resulting individual should be genetically identical with the donor of the nucleus—a partially man-made younger "identical twin." Microdissection feats of this order of complexity have already been performed with frog cells and might be possible in a few years with higher animals and even man. This would seem an excellent way to replicate successful race horses and prize bulls. However, revulsion and strong objections would without doubt arise if the technique were applied to human beings, and especially if any living young resulted from implanting a human nucleus in the womb of an animal such as a gorilla. Moreover the delicate operation would be liable to damage the embryo, leading to the problem of what to do with a physically or mentally deformed or even monstrous semisynthetic human being.

Many people will regard all such possibilities of viral transductions and "vegetative propogation" with distaste if not horror, and they may recall Macfarlane Burnet's warning, given in the previous chapter. Happily for them, there are reasons for believing that prospects for human genetic engineering are neither so promising as the optimistists hope, nor so hazardous as the pessimists fear. As explained in Chapter 13, human beings are able in large degree to transcend their inherited characteristics. Mental abilities and character owe far more to upbringing and education than to genetic factors, whether or not these can be artificially modified. Moreover, the sense of responsibility for the applications of science is increasing, and a growing social conscience is likely to prevent implementation of the more bizarre developments.

Anxiety about the hazards of genetic engineering is not groundless alarmism. Recently (July 1974) the National Academy of Science in America took the unprecedented step of appealing for a moratorium on certain specified kinds of research, and published this plea in both *Science* and *Nature*. The researches the Academy believes should be discontinued are those branches of genetic engineering directed toward introducing new genetic information into bacteria and viruses, because such variants could have unpredictable biological properties. They could be highly dangerous to animals and man, and the risk of accidental release is thought to present an unacceptable hazard.

Summary

Ordinary breeding programs represent interference with the natural course of heredity and could be regarded as genetic engineering. The term is normally restricted to deliberate manipulation of the genetic material in the cell nucleus. This is accomplished by mutagenic agents—radiation or certain chemicals—or by introducing new DNA carrying genetic information, usually by the agency of an infecting virus. Interference with heredity by the latter technique remains to be developed, but there is already evidence that it has occurred in plants, and also in human subjects, through laboratory accidents, fortunately without serious consequences. It is suggested that human genetic engineering is not such a fearsome prospect as some people believe.

REFERENCES

[1]F.L. Horsefall, *Science,* 1962, *136,* 472.
[2]L. Ledoux and R. Huart, *J. Molecular Biology,* 1969, *43,* 243.
[3]Stanfield Rogers, *New Scientist,* 1970 (Jan. 29), 194.

CHAPTER 12

EVOLUTION OF PLANTS AND ANIMALS

The orthodox Neo-Darwinian theory of evolution was briefly outlined in Chapter 9 and will not be elaborated further. Many thoughtful individuals are unable to accept an account of evolution that invokes only random and purely mechanistic processes; moreover, many eminent biologists are also dissatisfied with the present situation. The basic Darwinian theory is not in dispute, but it is believed to be incomplete; important factors that modify its operation are coming to light and there are probably others that remain to be discovered.

Directive Guidance of Evolution

In the 1950s Sinnott, Cannon, and others were writing about the integrating and directive control exercised by living organisms and the capacity for goal-seeking inherent in biological life. Thus Graham Cannon wrote:[1] "All the evidence points inexorably in one direction: to the conception of some guiding force within the organism which controls and guides its evolution, not by haphazard changes but by selected modifications." He went on to raise very fundamental doubts as to whether Mendelism was competent to bring about the major differentiations into species. He believed that the genes control only comparatively minor changes in organisms, and he invoked a second mechanism, which he called organismal control for the earlier and more extensive changes involved in the evolution of species. It may well be that such a mechanism operated before genes arose at all, well on in the evolutionary process (as suggested also in Chapter 8). Waddington, who does believe implicitly in the Mendelian theory, is nevertheless hard-put to explain how it can bring about all the many coordinated and integrated changes involved in the development of a new organ, for example. So he invokes a principle of harmonious control, a kind of supergene that orders the others to make things happen in the right manner. Such ideas do not seem very different from the outright teleology of the Greek philosophers, the notion that the world is a product of design, with a purposed end that controls the course of events. Darwinism was supposed to have discredited such beliefs, but they seem to be creeping back under new names.

The present purpose is to review a little of the more recent work in this field and to add a few comments in the light of ideas outlined in previous chapters. Sir Alister Hardy has written a most interesting book[2] based on his Gifford Lectures for 1963-64. In the second half of the book where he expounds his own views, Sir Alister is at pains to point out repeatedly that he is an orthodox Darwinian, except that he thinks the theory does not go far enough, and he wishes to graft on some additional mechanisms.

> As far as it goes, I completely accept this current view, but I do not believe it to be the whole story. There is another part of the process which I consider to be of equal or even greater importance. As to whether this other part is entirely physical, I am doubtful; . . . it is clear, however, that it must be closely linked with the physical process.

Sir Alister first points out that Lamarck has been misunderstood; he himself would have repudiated the crude notion of the inheritance of acquired characteristics that passes for Lamarckism today. Lamarckian effects are undoubtedly to be observed, but he was wrong as to the means; they are produced by pure Darwinian means—so everyone can be happy—and that is the main part of Sir Alister's thesis. Environment has its recognized selective effect, but a motile animal (unlike a plant) is also free to select his environment and what he will do there. He is free to change his habits, of locomotion or food-gathering for example, and if he does so, then there are bodily changes that would facilitate the new mode of living. In due course these changes come about in the species, not indeed as a *direct* result of the new need or the greater use of some organs, as Lamarck supposed, but through a succession of chance variations, and the perpetuation by natural selection of those that fitted in best with the changed habits. These are not entirely new ideas; Sir Alister has himself been brooding over them for twenty years or more, and he recognizes they are a development of the Organic Selection of Baldwin and Lloyd Morgan, and Waddington's principle of genetic assimilation, but he accords them a primary and not a mere secondary place in the evolutionary process.

> The gene combinations which are best suited to the *habits* of the animal may tend to survive in preference to those which do not give such full scope to the animal's pattern of behavior.

Natural Selection

Natural selection operates partly through adversities due to predators, competitors, and the environment. Predators are sometimes combatted successfully, especially among insects, by protective coloring and mimicry of unpalatable species. Competitors, whether of other species or rivals of the same species, tend to prevent the ill-adapted animal from getting enough food. The inanimate environment operates by such means as, for example, the selective value of thicker fur in cold climates.

> I would distinguish all the foregoing kinds under a super heading of *external* selective agencies, meaning those acting from outside the organisms concerned, i.e. the selective forces acting from both the animate and inanimate environments; and in contrast to these I would place an *internal* selective force due to the behavior and habits of the animal itself.

Numerous illustrations are given, including that of the great variation in the beaks of Darwin's finches on Galapagos.

Which is the more reasonable explanation of these adaptations: that chance mutations, first occurring in a few members of the population, caused these birds to alter their habits and seek new food supplies more suitable to their beaks and so become a more successful and surviving race, or did the birds, forced by competition, adopt new feeding habits which spread in the population so that chance changes in beak form giving greater efficiency came gradually to be preserved by organic selection?[2]

The same argument is applied to the much wider variations among beaks in general. The recent work of R.F. Ewer is mentioned with approval, and the following is quoted from one of her papers. Commenting on "the oversimplified teleology of an earlier unwarranted anthropomorphic attitude," she writes:

> The reaction against teleology was both natural and necessary but the trouble was, it went too far. In rejecting simple teleology it rejected teleology altogether; and in pointing out that no evidence was forthcoming for the inherited effects of an animal's own activity it concluded that the latter was an irrelevancy in evolutionary studies. . . . The concept of selective advantage is based on a consideration of "ends," although it does not place them inside the consciousness either of a creator or of the evolving animal and, as will become clear later, activities are very far from being irrelevant.

Telepathy

Another facet of Sir Alister's new ideas is the very tentative belief that these new habits may spread within an animal community by telepathy, or by communion with a sort of species unconscious (reminiscent of the notion of animal group souls). But Sir Alister introduces the idea apologetically and with the utmost timidity. He does, it is true, express firm belief in human telepathy (he is a Past President of the Society for Psychical Research), but he puts forward the extension to animals as the merest speculation, as likely to be wrong as right—though one senses that he believes in it himself.

> I have already explained that I am not a vitalist in the old-fashioned sense of believing that there is some vital force or

entelechy interfering directly with the physico-chemical reactions of the body in development. I am sure that the laws of physics and chemistry are never broken; yet . . . I am sure we have no right to assume that physics and chemistry as we at present understand them can explain the whole of life—particularly the body-mind relationship. . . . My "vitalism" is a belief that there is a psychic side of the animal which, apart from inherited instinctive behavior, may be independent of the DNA code that governs the form of the physical frame, but that it may interact with the physical system in the evolutionary process through organic selection.

In the scheme I am suggesting a sort of psychic pool of experience would be shared subconsciously by all members of a species by some method akin to what we are witnessing in telepathy. If such a highly speculative concept of a "racial plan" were true, then the old ideas of a "morph," "form" or "archetype" of the pre-evolutionary transcendentalists . . . might not seem quite so quaint as we have sometimes thought them; they might perhaps be the equivalent of what Jung has called the psychological archetype of his shared subconscious in the human species. Nevertheless, such a rash metaphorical speculation is, I believe, no more fanciful than some of the statements that are made with all the confidence of proven fact by some of our mechanistic biologists—such a statement, for example, as that. . . "We now find ourselves. . . reducing the *decisive controls* of life to a matter of the precise order in which the units are arranged in a giant molecule."[2]

L.L. Whyte has also written on internal factors in evolution;[3] indeed this is the title of his book, though he attaches a meaning to the phrase quite different from Sir Alister's. Like the latter, however, he has evidently been brooding over his ideas for many years, and he also has gathered up similar ideas that others have expressed less clearly and emphatically.

He points out that nineteenth century scientific thought "was influenced by the conception of *kinetic atomism,* of material units moving at random. The corresponding conception representative of the 20th century is that of *ordered structure,* of relatively stable arrangements of units." If this is true in physics, with its *quantized ordered states* of systems, it should be even more true of living forms. Therefore organisms need to be considered in terms of ordered structure, and not just as physicochemical systems.

Internal Selection

This has led him to propose another selective process in evolution, in addition to Darwinian selection.

> It is now being suggested that besides the well-established external competitive selection of the "synthetic" theory of evolution, an internal selection process acts directly on mutations, mainly at the molecular, chromosomal, and cellular levels, in terms not of struggle and competition, but of the system's capacity for co-ordinated activity. The Darwinian criterion of fitness for external competition has to be supplemented by another: that of good internal co-ordination. Internal co-adaptation is necessary as well as external adaptation.

> For any structural thinker must conclude that Darwinian adaptive selection has not been the only directive agency guiding the evolution of forms along the paths which they actually followed. The nature of life, the structural character of organisms, has itself imposed basic restrictions on the changes that are permissible. It has only been possible to neglect this natural conclusion because so little is yet known about this internal co-ordination which is "life." But once explicitly considered, this internal selection is seen to be just as natural and inevitable as Darwin's "natural selection."[3]

Whyte points out sadly that although new ideas travel quickly in physics, this does not seem to happen in the biological sciences, despite all the facilities for rapid communication. Thus although these ideas about internal selection may be almost commonplace to some molecular biologists, they are ignored or even actively denied by most leading biologists. "The struggles of the history of ideas are not over and done with in this age of conferences, grants, and travels."

Expressed in more detail, the idea is that mutations in the genic material do indeed occur in random fashion, but only a few of them survive the stringent coordinative conditions of the organism itself. Thus at the molecular level already, only a limited number of rearrangements will be stable within the gene, and of these only some will permit ordered chromosomal activities to continue, without loss of the faculty of replication, for example. The conditions for ontogenetic development (development of the individual organism), and those "which determine the unity of the entire genotype must place further restrictions on the potential for variation. . . . The conditions of biological organization restrict to a finite discrete spectrum the possible avenues of evolutionary change from a given starting point. The nature of life limits its variation and is one factor directing phylogeny (development of the species)."[3] Unsatisfactory mutations that do not pass the internal selection test may perhaps be eliminated in one of three ways. A return mutation may reestablish the *status quo;* the disturbed genotype may be reformed into something suitable; or if both are impossible, then it is one of the well-known lethal mutations that result in the death of cell or whole organism. Moreover "mutated genotypes which have passed internal selection will in certain circumstances have a positive correlation with the directions of evolution." Circumstances can be envisaged whereby during certain critical phases of evolution, internal selection alone may have been operative, the organisms meeting no adverse external conditions which would have weeded them out by normal Darwinian selection.

Both these books must be welcomed as attempts to break out from the thralldom of biology to that tempting twisting serpent, the DNA molecule. It seems appropriate to see life accorded a role in shaping vessels for its use. Sir Alister, and others whom he cites, have produced convincing evidence that animals can elect, or can be forced by a changing environment to adopt, new habits. His claim that bodily changes favorable to the new behavior will arise in Darwinian fashion seems inevitably true, once it is so clearly stated. The idea of telepathic spreading of new habits will be harder to establish, but seems reasonable—especially so perhaps in the light of two modern examples: the attacks of tits on milk-bottle tops to reach the cream, and of bullfinches on Daphne berries, spread throughout England within a year or so.

Whyte has summarized his proposition in the words: "The struggle for survival of mutations begins at the moment mutation occurs, but this is a 'struggle' to conform, not to compete." This also seems entirely reasonable once it is spelled out so clearly. It is a scheme that would avoid wastage; moreover freak animals are surely much more rare than might be expected on a basis of completely unchecked random mutations—though Whyte does not himself make these points.

Each author is saying in his own way that life must play some part in guiding evolution; one concentrates on the behavioral level, the other on that of cellular organization. Their ideas are complementary, not exclusive: both may well be right. These welcome additions to the mechanisms of evolution prompt the thought that there may well be still others waiting to be propounded. For it remains difficult to see how major changes involving many coordinated steps could have come about through a succession of random mutations, even though they may be screened by the Whyte mechanism; the reason is that creatures in half-way stages would be handicapped and less fit to survive than either the unmodified stock or the eventual new form.

Another factor that eases the restrictions imposed on the evolutionary process by strict Darwinism was propounded in stimulating fashion by A. Koestler.[4] He gives new prominence to a known but disregarded principle in biological evolution, and points out that it has a close parallel in mental evolution also. The paper concerns creativity, but since this is difficult to define, it is approached by way of contrast.

> The opposite of the creative individual is the pedant, the slave of habit, whose thinking and behavior move in rigid grooves. His biological equivalent is the over-specialized animal. Take, for example, that charming and pathetic creature, the koala bear, which specializes in feeding on the leaves of a particular variety of eucalyptus tree and on nothing else; and which, in lieu of fingers, has hook-like claws, ideally suited for clinging to the bark of the tree—and for nothing else. Some of our departments of higher learning seem expressly designed for breeding koala bears.

Retracing Steps in Evolution

Overspecialization has brought biological evolution almost to a standstill of stagnation or extinction. The orthodox idea is that evolution has proceeded via random mutations preserved by natural selection, and that it has led mainly to blind alleys from which the resulting highly specialized species cannot progress further. Koestler, however, suggests that there is an escape route, and moreover one that does not need to invoke any kind of divine intervention. It is via the well-established but neglected phenomenon of paedomorphism.

> It indicates that in certain circumstances evolution can retrace its steps, as it were, along the path which led to the dead-end and make a fresh start in a more promising direction. To put it simply, paedomorphism means the appearance of some evolutionary novelty in the larval or embryonic stage of the ancestral animal, a novelty which may disappear before the adult stage is reached, but which reappears in the adult descendant.[4]

This becomes possible through neotony, or gradual retardation of bodily development so that eventually breeding can take place at the more plastic larval or juvenile stage, leading to a rejuvenation and despecialization of the race.

> But of even greater importance than this re-winding of the biological clock is the fact that in the paedomorphic type of evolution selective pressure operates on the early, malleable stages of ontogeny. . . . One is accordingly led to expect that the major evolutionary advances were due to paedomorphism and not to gerontomorphism—to changes in the larval or embryonic, and not in the adult, stage.

By way of illustration, there is evidence that the chordates, and hence man, are descended from the larval stage of some primitive echinoderm, perhaps like the sea cucumber. The larvae are supposed to have evolved into more fishlike forms that eventually became sexually mature in this state, eliminating the old slug-like adult stage. Probably the last decisive evolutionary turning point marked by this necessary retracing of steps was when the line destined to become man branched off from some ancestral primate. This would explain why the human adult resembles so much more closely the embryo of an ape than the adult ape.

> It is as if the stream of life had momentarily reversed its course, flowing uphill for a while, then opened up a new streambed—leaving the koala bear stranded on its tree like a discarded hypothesis. We have now reached the crucial point in our excursion, because it seems to me that this process of *reculer pour mieux sauter*—of drawing back to leap, of undoing and re-doing—is a basic feature of all significant progress, both in biological and mental evolution.[4]

At a lower but still breathtaking level is an animal's power of self-repair or regeneration. A flatworm can grow again from a mere fragment, while amphibia can regenerate limbs and organs. This is done by regression of specialized tissues to a genetically less committed stage similar to the embryonic, followed by redifferentiation. This happens only when the traumatic challenge exceeds a critical limit, and is possible only by reverting to the genetic plasticity of the embryonic stage. Reversion to a larval stage, or what might be called phylogenetic "self-repair" is of course a much more extreme step leading to a new species better adapted to the critical challenge of a changing environment.

In man this capacity for physical regeneration is largely superseded by "the equally remarkable power of the nervous system to reorganize its mode of function." That is to say, the function of a damaged or excised portion of the brain can be taken over by another part.

Human Creativity

> But let us get on to man, and to those lofty forms of self-repair which we call self-realization, and which include creativity in its broadest sense. Psycho-therapy, ancient and modern, has always relied on 'regression in the service of the ego'. The neurotic with his compulsions, phobias and elaborate defense-mechanisms is a victim of maladaptive specialization—a koala bear hanging on for dear life to a barren tele-

graph pole. The therapist's aim is to regress the patient to an infantile or primitive condition; to make him retrace his steps to the point where they went wrong, and to come up again, metamorphosed, re-born. . . . All creative activity is a kind of do-it-yourself therapy, an attempt to come to terms with traumatizing experiences. In the scientist's case the trauma is . . . the sting of data which contradict each other, disrupt an established theory, and make nonsense of his cherished beliefs. The history of science, and of art too, is one of revolutionary successful escapes from blind alleys. There follow periods of consolidation, leading again to rigidity and orthodoxy, and eventually to a new crisis and another breakthrough. But while in retrospect the new direction appears natural enough, it was mental agony for the person who conceived it. To unlearn is more difficult than to learn; and it seems that the task of breaking up rigid cognitive structures and reassembling them into a new synthesis cannot, as a rule, be performed in the full daylight of the conscious, rational mind. It can only be done by reverting to those more fluid, less committed and specialized forms of ideation which normally operate in the twilight below the level of focal awareness. Such intervention of unconscious processes is now generally . . . accepted. [In the period of incubation] the creative individual experiences a temporary regression to patterns of thinking which are normally inhibited in the rational adult.[4]

Thus the analogy with biological systems appears close. To allow creativity in either, not only is temporary regression to an earlier condition necessary, but it has to be a more fluid and primitive one, quasi-embryological for the biological system, naive or juvenile for the mental, before creative potentials can be liberated, and with a cry of "Eureka!" escape from a blind alley is achieved. Moreover, in the evolution of ideas, as of species, progress is not continuous or strictly cumulative; the new is built, not upon the immediately preceding, but on something much further back along the line. "Biological evolution could be described as a history of escapes from over-specialization, the evolution of ideas as a series of escapes from mental habit; and the escape-mechanism in both cases is based on the same principles." Moreover, the comparison "points, however tentatively, at a common denominator, a factor of pur-

posiveness, without invoking a *deus ex machina*." Without denying the play of trial and error, this concept replaces the orthodox notion of complete randomness by
something much more complex and sophisticated: "a
groping and searching, retreating and advancing towards a
goal." As H.J. Muller has said: "Purpose is not imported
into Nature and need not be puzzled over as a strange or
divine something . . . it is simply implicit in the fact of organization." The ideas of goal-directedness or purpose
have become respectable, as biologists have become forced
to recognize that the facts of evolutionary progress simply
cannot be reconciled with blind chance.

> The part played by a lucky chance mutation is reduced to that
> of the trigger which releases the co-ordinated action of a
> system; and to maintain that evolution is the product of blind
> chance means to confuse the simple action of the trigger,
> governed by the laws of statistics, with the complex purposive
> processes which it sets off.
>
> Any directive process, whether you call it selective, adaptive or
> expectative, implies a reference to the future. The equifinality
> of developmental processes, the striving of the blastula to grow
> into an embryo, regardless of the obstacles and hazards to
> which it is exposed, might lead the unprejudiced observer to
> the conclusion that the pull of the future is as real and some-
> times more important than the pressure of the past.[4]

Koestler's paper evokes that "of course" response that
characterizes a brilliant intuitive perception. After all, we
can program our electronic computers to retrace their steps
when an impasse is reached. So it is inconceivable that
Nature, with all the complexity and adaptability she displays, should have been programmed with no reverse gear.

Nature is still busy working through the tail end of the
program, while man is taking over within the limits of his
capabilities, by planned crossings and culling by deliberate, instead of natural, selection. Thus man operates by
direct intervention; he has not yet learned to alter the program, though with his recent understanding of the genetic
code, this capability is not far off. It is worth noting, too,
that plant breeders have made some use of Koestler's prin-

ciple of *reculer pour mieux sauter*. For example, in order to introduce new and desired characteristics into wheat, they found it necessary to breed back to the primitive wheats still to be found in the wild in remote parts of the world; the required genes had been lost from all the cultivated varieties.

An End to Reductionism

It is abundantly clear that it is unreasonable to cling to the reductionist view that biological life will eventually become explicable *solely* by the laws of physics and chemistry. There is no suggestion that life *transgresses* these laws, but it does *transcend* them. Its higher order of organization is governed by additional laws of its own. As W.H. Thorpe points out,[5] even machines, much less bodies, are not *accounted for* by the laws of physics and chemistry. "The operational principles of living beings are embodied in the parameters left undetermined by physics and chemistry"—in the same way as machines. Even a machine "comprises at least two levels of existence in which the higher may rely on the lower without interfering with the laws governing the lower." Or as Polanyi puts it: "Biology explains living things in terms of mechanisms founded on the laws of physics and chemistry, but not determined by them."

As Thorpe says, in all such arguments it is essential to be on guard against what he calls "pseudo-substitution, which connotes the practice of surreptitiously stretching the meaning of terms in a more basic science to include ideas appropriate only to a higher science."

Thorpe continues his argument by the *reductio ad absurdum* approach. If one starts by assuming the mechanistic conception of the universe, its content of organized life nevertheless compels one to concede that this immense complexity could hardly have arisen by itself from randomness. So the final implication is a pattern of parameters within the primordial incandescent gas, which in turn implies abandoning randomness and with it the whole basis of thermodynamics. Even then sentience cannot be explained along these lines.

Information Theory

The appearance of new ideas is termed emergence. Information theory can provide some notion of the vast numbers of new ideas the appearance of life does entail; it cannot be precise, but it does give, at least to about an order of magnitude, a quantitative expression of the complexity of a system. Thus for example, a bacterial cell is specified by about 10^{12} binary digits (bits) of information. It is calculated that it uses some 10^9 bits per second during growth, and produces an additional 10^3 bits per second. The information content of the mature cell is greater by several orders of magnitude than that of the nucleic acid it originally contained. For comparison, some interesting figures on information contents are cited by Thorpe. For instance a symphony may contain some 4×10^7 bits, which come over at about 15,000 bits per second. A perfect picture on a color television screen may again comprise around 10^7 bits. The human brain in a lifetime may collect 10^{15} to 10^{20} bits of information. Some physical comparisons are the number of protons in the universe, put at 10^{80}, and the number of seconds elapsed during the existence of the galaxy, which is 10^{18} at most, an unexpectedly small number. "Some of these calculations are a most valuable corrective for some of those who argue about the high probability of the random origin of life in the Universe."[5]

Thorpe queries the possibility that all the information content of a living organism can be stored in the nucleus of the fertilized ovum. Unless the germ cell can store 10^{12} to 10^{15} bits within a space of radius two microns, then one has to ask whence comes the new information. The most elaborate computer made does not hold anywhere nearly so much information. Moreover the more it is microminiaturized the more trouble one has from interfering "thermal noise" due to random agitation of atoms. This has to be countered, at the expense of compactness, by redundancy, i.e. by introducing several bits of information for each one required in the final message, to ensure its perfection. The genetic code is enshrined not in electronic circuits but in the DNA double helix; it has been argued that its chemical bonds are highly resistant to thermal noise. Even so, there does not seem to be enough of it in the germ cell; but anyhow there is now a good deal of evidence that DNA is not alone responsible, and that cytoplasmic effects play a large part in the development of organisms. DNA cannot be the whole story of mechanical inheritance and may be only a small part of it (see Chapter 10).

Thorpe mentions that the bearing of his own conclusions on the argument for a universe from design is far-reaching, and that others have thought along these lines, but he refrains from revealing his own views.

Waddington,[6] has contributed further to the discussion of these problems, and has uncovered areas of confusion and slurring over of difficulties in the Neo-Darwinian approach, which differs fundamentally from that of Darwin himself. In the 1920s the most profound characteristic of living systems was considered to be their ability to increase local order by taking in simple molecules and arranging them into complex compounds and organic structures in an orderly fashion, whereas after death and in nonbiological nature generally when left to itself the reverse occurs and ordered systems tend to run down into a state of maximum disorder. However, these definitions ignore reproduction, i.e., the ability to pass on specificity from the initial unit to offspring. "For evolution to be possible something still further is required. It is necessary that changes occur from time to time in the specificity of an organism and that, when such changes occur, they are passed on to the offspring." This geneticist's definition of life is more general than the physiologists, and has become accepted. The reaction is, however, in danger of going too far. "To be worthy of being called alive . . . organisms must exhibit some sort of physiological activity." Life cannot be defined exclusively in terms either of the genotype, the repository of heredity, or of the phenotype, the living creature itself; both are involved.

Darwinism and Neo-Darwinism

Waddington points out that modern orthodox Neo-

Darwinism, although using the same phrases, has actually changed the meaning of almost all the words, so that what emerges is quite considerably different from what Darwin put forward. "Darwin was thinking of random phenotypic variation. Neo-Darwinism is thinking of random genotypic variation. Here neo-Darwinism is right, ... However, neo-Darwinism seems to me to be wrong in so far as it usually tacitly assumes that randomness of genetic mutation implies randomness of phenotypic variation."[6] As Kety remarked, discussing another of Waddington's papers[7] "it is the phenotype which competes with the environment, but it is the genotype which is transmitted. It is one of those self-evident things that become self-evident only when someone has pointed it out." The phenotype does not consist merely of proteins corresponding to all the genes, and nothing else. "It is instead made up of a highly heterogeneous assemblage of parts, in each of which there are some, but not all, of the proteins for which the genes could serve as patterns, and in each of which there are also many other substances and structures over and above the primary proteins corresponding to particular genes."[7] A basic tenet of information theory is that information cannot arise by itself, but it seems obvious that a living animal contains more information than the egg-cell. "Information" remains a useful term, employed loosely.

Turning to the concept of survival of the fittest, Waddington points out that Darwin appeared to think of survival as meaning a long life, while "fittest" meant for him "most able to carry out the ordinary transactions of life."

> The neo-Darwinist meaning is quite different. For survival they substitute—quite rightly—reproduction; and by fittest they mean "most effective in contributing gametes to the next generation." Thus the whole consideration of ability to carry out the ordinary business of life has disappeared from the neo-Darwinist theory, and is replaced entirely by the conception of reproductive efficiency. This in effect reduces Darwinism to a tautology, and leaves for quite separate discussion—which is very rarely provided—why animals should have evolved all

sorts of highly adaptive structures to do unlikely things instead of being reduced to bags of eggs and sperm like certain
parasitic worms.[6]

Random Search or Guidance

It seems to be generally agreed among orthodox biologists that the essential process of evolution is dependent
on random search. Examples are quoted, with some calculations that seem to show that random search and natural
selection in mutable, self-replicating populations is totally
inadequate to account for the complexity of organisms.
Waddington in effect concedes this point, and argues that
biology is not in fact tied to the notion of random search.
Most random single gene mutations produce negligible or
harmful effects.

> In the production of a phenotype efficient at some task impor-
> tant to natural selection, such as, in horses, running fast to
> escape from enemies, or being able to feed on tough or low-
> growing herbage, very many genes will be concerned.

> Let us suppose that some environmental change puts a natural
> selective pressure on a population of Drosophila to increase
> the speed of its flight. There are at least 6 genes known that
> alter the mechanical or geometrical properties of the thorax,
> which would affect amplitude of wing-beat. Others must alter
> the properties of muscles, or the supplies of enzymes or sub-
> strates providing energy. Many known genes affect wing size,
> shape and aerodynamic properties, flexibility, etc. It is from
> this large array of possibilities that natural selection has to find
> some solution or other that brings about an increase in the
> speed of the insect's flight. This is a very different task from
> that envisaged in the phrase "random search," which is
> usually taken to imply that the population has to wait for a
> new gene to turn up which produces by itself a more or less
> specific effect which natural selection is demanding."[6]

This certainly seems to admit goal-directed selection.
Natural selection demands a result, and has to find some solution or other to achieve it. To abandon random search is
surely to accept some guiding principle, but Waddington
seems to avoid coming to grips with this problem.

It has even been suggested that the whole theory of natural selection involves tautological reasoning—arguing in circles, proving nothing. Ludwig von Bertalanffy refers to this criticism in his contribution to *Beyond Reductionism*.[7] He concedes that selection appears competent to explain many examples, but takes exception to the claim that the theory furnishes *in principle* a *complete* explanation of evolution. There are innumerable examples of structures and behavior that cannot really be seen to have any selective advantage. Indeed, it has sometimes been said that "the principle of selection is a tautology. It is in the sense that the selectionist explanation is always a construction *a posteriori*. Every surviving form, structure or behavior—however bizarre, unnecessarily complex or outright crazy it may appear—must, *ipso facto*, have been viable or of some 'selective advantage,' for otherwise it would not have survived. But this is no proof that it was a product of selection."

> Furthermore, selection *presupposes* self-maintenance, adaptability, reproduction, etc. of a living system. These therefore cannot be the *effects* of selection. This is the oft-discussed circularity of the selectionist argument. . . .

> I think the fact that a theory so vague, so insufficiently verifiable and so far from the criteria otherwise applied in "hard" science, has become a dogma, can only be explained on sociological grounds. Society and science have become so steeped in the ideas of mechanism, utilitarianism and the economic concept of free competition, that instead of God, Selection was enthroned as the ultimate reality.[7]

Nonacceptance of orthodox Darwinism is probably more widespread among younger academics than is generally realized. They hesitate to speak out for fear of damaging their prospects, so it is only the established men who are prepared to challenge the Establishment openly. For example, the eminent entomologist W.R. Thompson wrote in an introduction to the centenary edition of Darwin's *Origin of Species:*

> This situation, where scientific men rally to the defense of a

doctrine they are unable to define scientifically, much less demonstrate with scientific rigor, attempting to maintain its credit with the public by the suppression of criticism and the elimination of difficulties, is abnormal and undesirable in science. Thus are engendered those fragile towers of hypotheses based on hypotheses, where fact and fiction mingle in an inextricable confusion.[8]

The combined weight of all these arguments leads inexorably to the conclusion that is the foundation of this book, namely the existence of a nonmaterial information matrix and some kind of incorporeal guidance of evolution.

Summary

The Darwinian theory is right as far as it goes but it is inadequate as a complete explanation of evolutionary events. An animal is free to select his environment and feeding habits. In due course bodily changes occur that facilitate the new mode of living, by Darwinian means though they simulate the discredited Lamarckian mechanism. Changes in living habits may spread telepathically. Another kind of internal selection in evolution may act directly upon mutations at the cellular level such that only those survive which are favorable to the internal coordination which is life.

Overspecialization blocking further evolutionary progress may sometimes be circumvented by reversion to a more primitive and plastic stage such as the larval from which a fresh start can be made.

Darwin's theory has been altered greatly by according new meanings to its original terms: it is arguable that its new form is merely tautologous, arguing in circles.

The reductionist view that life is in principle explicable solely by the laws of chemistry and physics has become untenable. Life does not transgress these laws but it does transcend them. The amount of information manifestly increases enormously as evolution proceeds, and nonphysical intelligence seems to be its only conceivable source.

REFERENCES

[1]H. Graham Cannon, *The Evolution of Living Things,* Manchester University Press, 1958.

[2]Sir Alister Hardy, *The Living Stream—Evolution and Man,* Collins, London, 1965.

[3]L.L. Whyte, *Internal Factors in Evolution,* Tavistock Publications, London, 1965.

[4]A. Koestler, *Nature,* 1965, *208,* 1033.

[5]W.H. Thorpe, *Science, Man and Morals,* Cox & Wyman, London, 1965.

[6]C.H. Waddington, Contributions to an IUBS Symposium at Bellagio, Italy, 1966.

[7]A. Koestler and J.R. Smythies, *Beyond Reductionism,* Hutchinson, London, 1969.

[8]W.R. Thompson, Introduction to Centenary Edition of Darwin's *Origin of Species,* Everyman Library, No. 811, Dent, London, 1956.

CHAPTER 13

HUMAN EVOLUTION

At last the long march of evolution brought forth the human form, distinguished by its upright stance, jaw, and facial features and large brain with developed frontal lobes. Man is also unique in being relatively nonspecialized; most other species came to a dead end through overspecialization of limbs or feet for special limited purposes (see Chapter 12), but man's animal ancestors contrived to avoid this trap. Repeated fossil finds have pushed back the date of emergence of Homo sapiens to at least one million years ago and to several millions for more primitive hominids. But this is recent in geological terms, for it has to be compared with four thousand million years for the age of the earth as a planet and nearly three thousand million years for the emergence of the first known living organisms. To transpose these figures to a more apprehensible time scale, we may divide them by 10 million and so imagine the earth to be four hundred years old. The first primitive organisms would have emerged some three hundred years ago and Homo sapiens only a month ago. The earliest known civilizations go back only two days and advanced technology ten minutes. According to the prophets of doom, humanity may last out only a few more minutes on this time scale.

Biological Evolution Ending

By the time of man's arrival on the scene the evolutionary stream had come nearly to a halt. No major new species are known to have emerged during the last few million years; such changes as have taken place naturally, i.e. without human intervention, have been relatively minor variations in color and other superficial features. Yet during this period, or rather during the last small portion of it, man himself has evolved at a phenomenal rate, for civilized technological man is like a new species in relation to the primitive savage. However, this change owes nothing whatever to his genetics, for natural genetical change is an exceedingly slow process which could not operate at anything like this rate. Besides, it is clear that all this progress has been brought about by man himself; it is a product of the human mind, spirit, and will, not of biology. This has been well understood in some departments of human affairs but because biologists are so deeply committed to thinking in terms of genetics they have been slow to recognize the facts, and some of them even today write as if man were still at the mercy of his heredity. Sir Julian Huxley was one of the first biologists to point out that man has his own unique mode of evolution which he called psychosocial evolution. Man does not have to pass on his achievements by somehow impressing them upon his genetic apparatus for transmission to his children; instead he can pass them on immediately by word of mouth or by writing, and not only to his own children but to anyone who is interested. All this is possible because man is unique among living creatures in having invented language (see Chapter 3). As Julian Huxley put it, "Man's evolution is not biological but sociological. It operates by the mechanism of cultural tradition which involves the cumulative self-reproduction and self-variation of mental activities and their products."[1]

Aggression

Many biologists however still insist that we have inherited from animal ancestors our less agreeable traits, the most dangerous of which are our aggressive characteristics. Popular books that have expounded this theme forcefully and have had wide circulation have been written by Ronald Ardrey (*The Territorial Imperative*)[2] and Desmond

Morris (*The Naked Ape*).[3] Other writers, among whom are Bertrand Russell[4] and Sigmund Freud,[5] trace back an aggressive "instinct" in man not necessarily to the animal world, but to savage human ancestors. Both groups believe that aggressive behavior patterns in animals or primitive man became established through their survival value, and were genetically transmitted to humanity. They persist and govern our behavior because aggression still has survival value to man. According to Morris,

> . . . the basic pattern of behavior that we inherit is that of the predatory descendants of the peaceful fruit-eating and tree-dwelling apes who descended to the ground and became hunters. This transition involved radical changes, both in the anatomy, the habits, the sexual life, and the behavior pattern of the new tribal animal. These were established by variations which were established by their survival value passed on by inheritance. We ourselves are determined by them since civilization is so recent that too little time has elapsed to change our biological inheritance.

If aggression were indeed genetically determined, then there would be little hope for mankind. Unfortunately this notion has become popular lately, thanks in part to books like *The Naked Ape*. It is ultimately a philosophy of despair but meanwhile offers some comfort; if our baser nature is set by our genes then it isn't really our fault and we can be excused for our wrongdoing. "You can't change human nature"—and indeed you couldn't if it truly were so deep-rooted. But happily this is not so; human nature is changing all the time. Man is unique and his behavior is not in the main controlled genetically.

Lewis and Towers have taken the unusual step of publishing a book called *Naked Ape or Homo Sapiens*[6] as a direct refutation of the arguments of Desmond Morris and the other authors cited, showing that their arguments have no proper scientific basis; they depend upon analogies and hypotheses that cannot be supported by unbiased consideration of the evidence. Lewis and Towers start by declaring roundly that man is not an ape nor is he naked. The genealogical lines that led from some primitive ancestral type to the apes on the one hand and to man on the other probably diverged more than thirty million years ago, and no subsequent direct connection is recognized by science. Secondly, man has actually *more* hairs per unit area than other primates and most mammals, but they are mainly fine sensitive hairs, not a rug to keep him warm.

We are definitely not descended from the anthropoid apes so therefore none of our characteristics can have been inherited from them. Moreover "hunting does not imply internecine war, aggression, and ferocity. Hunting communities like the Eskimos are entirely peaceful and co-operative. People living on grain and eating hardly any meat at all have proved just as capable of becoming warlike and predatory as those who live by hunting."[6] This view is strongly supported by Bernard Campbell,[7] who writes:

> Anthropology teaches us clearly that man lived at one with nature until, with the beginnings of agriculture, he began to tamper with his ecosystem: an expansion of his population followed. It was not until the development of the temple towns (around 5,000 B.C.) that we find evidence of inflicted death and warfare. This is too recent an event to have had any influence on the (biological) evolution of human nature. Man is not programmed to kill and make war, nor even to hunt: his ability and desire to do so are learnt from his elders and his peers when his society demands it.

Man Controls his own Evolution

In the main man is guided not by instinct but by reason. He decides rationally what he wants, and plans his actions in order to attain his chosen ends. Whereas the animal must make what use he can of nature as he finds it, man imposes his will on nature, changing it deliberately to suit his purposes. As Campbell puts it:

> For a long time now, anthropologists have recognized that the principal means of man's adaptation has been cultural: *those beliefs, customs and practices that are learnt.* The animal roots of human nature determine man's potential: his culture realizes it.

But we may take this idea further, for in fact man often transcends his genetically inherited potential. Human intelligence, drawing upon cosmic intelligence for inspiration, plans to achieve more than muscles can accomplish; so then man invents machines and harnesses the power of wind, water, or fossil fuels to drive them. He introduces technology and complex social and economic organization. This kind of evolution is entirely different from and enormously quicker than biological evolution.

> In man we reach a new stage, that of non-genetical transmission by brains that allows him to *teach* and to *learn*. This is a new form of heredity not based on chromosomes but on *learnt* information, passed on by tradition. . . . Social, cultural and technological evolution must be sharply distinguished from the genetical form. . . . It therefore misses the point entirely to say, as Morris does, that the period of civilization has not been long enough "to make any substantial difference to man's genetical make-up."[6]

The point is that once man has become civilized genetics simply do not enter into the situation any longer. Man "transcends all genetically inherited animal characteristics and takes charge of these, utilizing them, modifying them and dominating them, until they can be virtually disregarded as having any *independent* influence upon behavior."[6]

Koestler[8] has put forward a different view of man's failings. He does not relate them to man's animal ancestry but does nevertheless propose that they are built-in genetically. He argues that "during the last explosive stages of the evolution of homo sapiens, something has gone wrong; that there is a flaw, some subtle engineering mistake built in to our native equipment which would account for the paranoid streak running through our history." He refers to this supposed flaw as a "species-specific disorder of behavior." But as Campbell points out:

> The idea that something can go wrong in evolution is meaningless. . . . Evolution does not "make mistakes": evolution is the most creative process in the universe. . . . Man's condition is not and cannot be accounted for by postulating an inbuilt flaw. . . . If our errors are cultural, not biological, this is

grounds for optimism: but it also means we cannot blame any-one but ourselves. To blame the state of affairs on our biology is not only dangerously irresponsible; it has no basis in fact.

Nevertheless, there is something in what Koestler says, even if his terminology is at fault on this occasion. As noted in Chapter 4, man's progress toward harmony and altru-ism is indeed retarded by something in his past—the in-stincts associated with the old brain. In crowds aroused by emotional events, for example, the prefrontal lobes are put to sleep, so to speak, the animal brains take over and the crowd becomes a mob.

Even at the biochemical level, man has learnt to over-come his genetic disabilities. The wide choice of marriage partners available in most communities ensures a complex reassortment of genes at each mating such that no two in-dividuals in the world are completely identical; extrachro-mosomal inherited factors (see Chapter 10) make this true even for "identical twins" derived from division of a single fertilized ovum. We are familiar with differences in height, build, features, coloration, fingerprints and so on, but it is less well known that differences occur also within the body. The internal organs may vary in size over an astonishing range, and also their positions may differ within the body cavity. So also the rates of production of the body's numer-ous enzymes (see Chapter 9) can vary over a surprisingly large range from one individual to another. In some persons, vital enzymes may be seriously deficient or may even be missing altogether, and this may affect the indi-vidual's health, his ability to digest and utilize certain foods, and so forth.

By not inertly accepting the situation he can do some-thing to adapt his way of life to the idiosyncracies of his in-dividual make-up. By experiment and experience it is pos-sible to discover a suitable diet, in terms both of what to eat and drink and what to avoid; this gives point to the saying that "one man's meat is another man's poison." Of course we are not always sufficiently wise or strong-willed to con-trol our diets in the way that would be best for our health; we are apt to sacrifice future well-being for present pleasure, and to overeat or take delicious foods or drink that we know will disagree with us. In extreme circumstances biochemical knowledge can be invoked to devise special diets to circumvent the ill-effects that would otherwise arise from lack of a particular enzyme, a so-called inborn error of metabolism, like phenylketonuria, a fault in the metabolism of aromatic amino acids that can lead to mental deficiency. Another example is the disease galactosaemia that afflicts some infants. The sugar lactose that is present in all kinds of milk is hydrolized by the enzyme lactase into glucose and galactose. These particular infants cannot metabolize galactose because they lack the enzyme that breaks it down, and for them it acts as a poison. These babies can only be reared safely on a diet from which all animal milk is replaced by plant milk made from nuts and soya beans.

Again, one person may benefit from strenuous exercise while another should be cautious. Different systems of healing too can be tested when necessary, because what is best for some individuals may not suit others. The powerful modern drugs represent a special hazard; a dose that is barely enough for one person may be nearly lethal for a second. The "average man" is a mathematical myth; almost all real people differ widely from the average in most respects.

One Humanity

There is another respect in which we could with advantage transcend inherited differences, but often fail to do so. This concerns our attitude toward race. Ethnic groups do differ to some degree in their internal biochemistry and externally in such evident ways as skin color and type of features and hair. However striking these differences may be, they are relatively minor and superficial. Indeed the total of genetic differences between, say, African Negroes and Anglo-Saxons is probably less than those which exist within either of these breeding populations. In particular, and despite statements to the contrary, it seems to have been abundantly proved that *inherent* mental abilities do not differ significantly between ethnic groups. Within any group the I.Q.s (intelligence quotients) vary over a considerable range, and these differences *within* an ethnic group are far greater than the differences *between* group averages. Actual *realized* mental abilities are indeed lower in some members of the colored groups, but this is due to their underprivileged position and poor educational facilities. When opportunities are equal from an early age, so also are average intellectual achievements. Since human evolution derives predominantly from culture and not from genetics, it may reasonably be stated that mankind comprises in effect one single race. Any antipathies we may experience towards ethnic groups other than our own are irrational and are not inherited, but arise from cultural and indoctrinated prejudices. The world would be a happier place if we could all bring ourselves to accept and act upon these facts.

Man's Responsibilities

Humanity must now come to terms with itself. Man's urgent need is to become actively aware of the fact that he has transcended his heredity, has taken charge of his own destiny, and can no longer put the blame for his shortcomings upon biology.

It has already become a commonplace that man has brought to bear upon the development of the earth's resources such greed and cupidity as would be unbelievable if it had not actually happened. Indeed the idea is now so familiar that it fails to shock or to engender much sense of guilt. Earlier centuries saw the callous exploitation of labor and the accumulation of wealth by a small ruling class. It must be admitted, however, as Sir Kenneth Clark brings out in his book and 1971 television series *Civilization*[9] that this arrangement did permit a development of culture, art, and science that could never have come about in a truly egalitarian society. All too familiar is the recent history of the industrial revolution and the resulting exploitation of man by man and of nation by nation, the development of terrible armaments and their use in disastrous wars, and the ever-increasing pollution of the earth. We are indeed awakening to all these evils, but we are still not prepared to pay the price to put them right, which is a temporary reduction in our standard of living.

There are signs that individuals and governments are waking up to the enormity of mankind's rape of the planet; extensive action is already planned, though not yet on a sufficiently comprehensive scale. Correspondingly, the prophets of doom are becoming more optimistic and constructive. Three examples must suffice. In 1960 a paper in *Science*[10] predicted that a "standing room only" situation of "infinite" world population would be reached within the lifetime of children already born, namely by the year 2026. This conclusion was reached by crude extrapolation of population trends and involved inadmissible assumptions, as correspondents pointed out. But its deliberate shock tactics did serve to focus attention on the problem. In contrast *Population, Resources, Environment* by Paul and Anne Ehrlich, published in 1970[11] is a large volume, extremely fully documented, with tables, diagrams, and references. Broadly its theme is to delineate the areas in which urgent action is imperative if ultimate disaster is to be avoided. Finally, in 1971, Ehrlich published, with Harriman, another book[12] providing detailed analyses of the required legislation, national and international.

Among Ehrlich's many interesting conclusions perhaps the most striking and devastating is his assertion that it is Western man and especially American man who constitutes the main threat to the planet. This is because of his ruthless exploitation of scarce resources to satisfy his greed for material possessions, all with planned obsolescence and packed in "disposable" containers. Accordingly it is argued that checking population growth is a much more vital problem for developed than for undeveloped countries, intrinsically as well as to set an example.

In technologically developed countries with democratic governments, men go on strike to improve their material standard of living. Yet for even the most poorly paid workers in these countries it is already too high in relation to standards in most Eastern countries. Our materialistic culture is sustained only at the expense of disastrous running-down of the earth's reserves of metal bearing ores and fossil fuels, and by industries creating intolerable pollution of land, water, and air. It is fortunate, ecologically speaking, that inflation soon neutralizes most of the wage and salary increments. Already there is no hope whatever of all the developing nations reaching their promised goal of a North American or even a European standard of industrial development. The world population is doomed by its sheer numbers to perpetual division into "haves" and "have-nots," unless the Western world voluntarily disciplines itself to accept a simpler way of life. "The people who bear the responsibility for saving Spaceship Earth are the first class passengers."[12]

Professor Sorokin was writing in 1941[13] about what he called our sensate culture, and the need to develop more concern for the quality of life and to relinquish some of our greed for material possessions. Our goal of an ever-increasing materialistic standard of living is a mistaken one. New cultural values need to be encouraged, which are meaningful for a simpler and more satisfying way of life and which tend to develop man's innate potentials. Exhortations such as Sorokin's are still valid more than thirty years later, even though they have been heeded by only a minority of individuals in Western countries.

By thus usurping the powers of the gods, man has inescapably taken upon himself the most terrible responsibilities. This may be said to mark his coming of age, when he has to forego the irresponsibilities of youth and the shelter of the parental home and accept his manhood. It marks, too, a changing attitude toward religion. In Christian terms he now deliberately rejects the guiding hand of God the Father and for the moment he stands alone. Yet he knows in his heart that he need not; his only salvation now is to become one with God the Holy Spirit. In more practical terms, man is not rejecting religion itself but its outer form that he no longer needs, namely organized religion and the power of priestcraft; he will now seek religion for himself. But fearful to take this bold step, he tends to acknowledge his weakness by merely shifting his allegiances. He transfers from faith in the priest to faith in "Them," in the scientist and in the statesman who promises an earthly paradise. But we are all in this together, and none can escape his share of the responsibility. If we have made a mess of running our planet—as indeed we have—there is no one to blame but ourselves, and no one to put it right but ourselves. Inspiration we may seek and receive but we have to translate it into effective action by our own human intelligence. Enlightened individuals may continue to arrive amongst us, but they will remain largely ineffective unless we heed them and see that they rise to positions of power. By entering into our common heritage we may come to realize what we already are in essence, if not in external fact, godlike humanity. Only thus may we come to peace on earth and the good life.

Summary

Biological evolution virtually ended with man's emergence. His own continuing evolution is not genetic but along cultural, technological, and social lines, its speed made possible by man's mental abilities and use of language. Progress tends to be held back, not—as some biologists have supposed—by specific aggressive instincts inherited from animal or human ancestors, but rather by the conflict between the old animal brain and humanity's new brain. Much technological and social organization has been irresponsible, and future harmony is critically dependent upon sincere acceptance of total responsibility toward our fellows and our planet.

REFERENCES

[1] Julian S. Huxley, *The Humanist Frame*, Allen and Unwin, London 1961.
[2] Robert Ardrey, *The Territorial Imperative*, Collins, London 1967.
[3] Desmond Morris, *The Naked Ape*, Cape, London 1967.
[4] Bertrand Russell, *Authority and the Individual*, Allen and Unwin, London 1948.
[5] Sigmund Freud, *Civilization and Its Discontents*, Hogarth Press, London 1929.
[6] John Lewis and Bernard Towers, *Naked Ape or Homo Sapiens*, Garnstone Press, London 1969.
[7] Bernard Campbell, *New Scientist*, 22 Oct. 1970, 184.

[8]Arthur Koestler, *Chemistry in Britain*, April 1970.

[9]Sir Kenneth Clark, *Civilization*, B.B.C. and John Murray, London 1971.

[10]H. von Foerster, P.M. Mora, and L.W. Amiot, *Science*, 1960, *132*, 1291; 1962, *136*, 173.

[11]Paul and Anne Erhlich, *Population, Resources, Environment*, W.H. Freeman, London 1970.

[12]Paul Ehrlich and Richard Harriman, *How to be a Survivor: a Plan to Save Spaceship Earth,* Ballantine Books, New York 1971.

[13]A. Sorokin, *The Crisis of Our Age*, E.P. Dutton, New York 1941.

CHAPTER 14

TOWARD A SYNTHESIS

The human brain without doubt represents the pinnacle in the evolution of organized forms on this planet; but it is not the pinnacle of human evolution. Contrary to what some materialistic biologists would have us believe, the essential man is an immaterial spiritual being who uses the brain along with the rest of the body to unfold his inner faculties. This is the theme of Section One of this book. But again, contrary to what most scientists believe, or affect to believe, the rational mind of man that functions through the brain still does not represent the highest point of human evolution, as Chapter 6 points out. Beyond the rational mind, from some realm called by Northrop the aesthetic continuum, man derives his feeling nature, his capacity to appreciate beauty in nature and art, his regard for ethical values, his spiritual aspirations, and his intuitive and mystical insights.

These last elements of man's consciousness are apt to disturb and confuse him because they are not biddable like the rational mind. Their intimations often come unsought and are sometimes even unwelcome. Intuition cannot be commanded; only when the proud rational mind is humble and still, submissive to something greater than itself, can the flash of inspiration come with its compelling intensity. The mystic is seized by a deeper transcendent experience; he touches the source of inspiration itself and is briefly absorbed into union with this universal wisdom and power. This is no illusion. On the contrary, it is the most vivid and convincing experience the individual can ever know. It cannot be denied or set aside, and while the memory lasts it may be powerful enough to change his whole life pattern. Mystical experience is still not very common, but the combined testimonies of an enormous number of people altogether suffice to establish the reality of this One Life, or Cosmic Intelligence, or whatever inadequate name one gives to it.

Sections Two and Three of this book are concerned with the coming of life to our planet and the ordered complexity of the ensuing living forms which compels one to postulate some intelligent guiding principle in nature, some nonmaterial information matrix. It is reasonable to conclude that it is this same Intelligence with which we make halting contact in the mystical experience.

This book does not concern itself with the earlier and more fundamental problem of the origin of the material universe, the creation of the elementary particles, their assembly into chemical elements and their compounds and then into galaxies, suns, and planets. In this realm there has been no shortage of testimony to the need for intelligent guidance. Astronomers in particular have often been inspired by the majesty of the heavens to philosophize in this sense. From an earlier generation one may cite the familiar works of Jeans and Eddington. More recently (1967) Firsoff[1] suggested that "mind is a universal entity or interaction of the same order as electricity or gravitation," and that "there must exist a *modulus of transformation*, analogous to Einstein's famous equation $E=mc^2$ whereby 'mind stuff' can be equated with other entities of the physical world." (See also end of Chapter 8.)

In Section Two, accordingly, the book makes a fresh start by looking, not all the way back to the creation of the universe, but to that era over 3000 million years ago when the earth made its long preparations to nurture living things. In Chapter 7 it is conceded that the materials of life, those relatively simple chemical compounds used by organized forms to build the complex molecules which compose their cells, could have been produced by nonbiological agencies.

Thus it is reasonable to suppose that a considerable range of such compounds became dissolved in pools of water on the primitive earth. This "prebiotic soup," as it has been called, could doubtless have nourished appropriate micro-organisms. But it is quite another thing to suppose, as many materialistic scientists do, that the mere presence of these nutrients was enough to insure that living forms would somehow create themselves *ab initio* out of this material. This is like suggesting that to produce motor cars it is only necessary to bring together lumps of various metals and other materials and leave them to construct and assemble themselves! We know very well that this would not happen no matter how many millions of years we allowed for the process. Yet some people profess to believe that living organisms *could* have arisen spontaneously, although even the most primitive imaginable is far more complex than a car, in terms of the number of unit components.

This miracle of life could not possibly have happened through lucky chance aggregations. Chapter 8 brings together numerous considerations to support this statement. Unfortunately, observation and experiment are not directly applicable to events so far in the past. However, it is a matter of observation and in accord with the laws of probability that complex ordered schemes do not emerge of themselves from chaos. It may be argued that small ordered fragments might happen to come together by chance at infrequent intervals, and that if they could be segregated by some mechanism, some few of them might happen to fit together into larger fragments displaying significant order for the construction of living forms. But it is farfetched to imagine a long succession of such accidents adequate to put together a living primitive organism—as farfetched as to find the pieces of a jumbled jigsaw puzzle assembling themselves.

Anyhow, what mechanism can be suggested, apart from intelligent selection, to pick out the ordered fragments from the vastly greater mass of chemical rubbish? However distasteful the idea may be to materialists, there is really no escape from intelligent guidance, from what is here called a nonmaterial information matrix.

The third Section of the book traces the gradual evolution of these early primitive organisms into the more complex plants and animals of today, and the eventual emergence of man with his unique highly developed brain. Darwinism and Neo-Darwinism are alike shown to be inadequate; they need not be rejected, but they are totally insufficient by themselves to account for all the variety of evolved forms. The difficulty is that at every step, at every transformation of one species into another, a lot more information is added to the system. And, as noted earlier, information cannot arise by itself; it cannot be inherent in inorganic matter, in the chemical atoms, so it must be imported from some nonmaterial source. There really seems no escape from this conclusion whichever way one turns and however much one may desire mechanistic explanations. To reiterate the conclusion reached in Chapter 12, it is imperative to postulate a nonmaterial information matrix for genetic guidance. This is tantamount to saying that the intelligent guidance came first; it was not the product of evolution but was itself the prime cause of evolution. As successive organisms developed they expressed this intelligence more and more fully in the physical world.

The modern science of molecular biology, which professes to provide a mechanistic explanation of life, reveals previously unsuspected complexities of ordering at the molecular level, and thus only succeeds in making it much more difficult to understand in mechanical terms, unless one turns a prejudiced blind eye to the obvious implications. The ancient concept of undifferentiated protoplasm as a filling for cells is replaced by an incredibly elaborate array of highly structured organelles, each with its own special metabolic function. Even the macromolecules of which they are composed are anything but random aggregations of simpler molecules, but contain precisely ordered sequences. To pretend that all this arose through the working of blind chance, over however many aeons, seems obvious nonsense. Thus the further the molecular biologists go in revealing these intricacies, the more untenable they render their own mechanistic interpretations.

The case for a guiding Cosmic Intelligence has been stated and consolidated, but so far no consideration has been given to the manner in which it might interact with matter, whether animate or inanimate. In common experience, human intelligence has no direct effect upon external objects. A few people, it is true, have claimed success in psychokinesis experiments (see Chapter 2), but the possibility is not widely accepted. Again, at numerous spiritualistic seances, objects (apports) have appeared suddenly, brought by no evident physical means of transportation, sometimes from a known distant place.

If these phenomena in fact occur, the mechanism by which they do so is highly significant. Inadequate research still permits doubt as to the facts in these two examples of external influence, but there can be no doubt whatever as to the effect of mind on matter *within* living organisms. No one denies that a thought or a feeling can result in vigorous motion of material limbs. Here human intelligence is translated into physical action in our own bodies every moment of our waking lives. Biologists have explained how nerve impulses trigger muscular contractions, but the earlier all-important step by which thought produces the nerve impulse remains a mystery. By analogy Cosmic Intelligence may similarly be capable of influencing physical events in the whole natural world, which in some mysterious way can be regarded as its "body." It is impossible to formulate the hypothesis with any precision, but this is not surprising when we cannot even explain the interaction between human thought and nerve impulses.

However improbable it may seem, there is overwhelming evidence for intelligent guidance in nature, so there just has to be some mechanism for its interaction with living forms. It is a question not of wondering whether this is possible, but of how it can come about. Several philosophers have considered the problem, including, for example, the physicist Schrödinger in his little book, *What is Life?*[2] He made the point that interactions need only be envisaged at atomic or molecular levels, where some indeterminacy is allowed by the laws of physics. At first sight, the idea of mind acting directly upon "matter," as we commonly regard it, does seem to pose formidable problems. But if instead we regard matter in the way that modern physics does, namely as something like a conglomeration of minute whirling bundles of energy, then the difficulty is lessened. For if we may regard thought also as a kind of energy (as Firsoff has hinted[1]) then the phenomenon is reduced to the interaction of like with like. Indeed it is reasonable to go further and to suggest that matter, in this modern immaterial sense, is pervaded by intelligence. Thus by starting from scientific observations and theories, and applying logical deductions, one arrives, as did Schrödinger, at the position taken, for example, by Hinduism—itself originally derived from direct mystical understanding. As it is expressed poetically in the Bhagavad Gita: "Having pervaded this whole universe with one fragment of Myself, I remain."[3]

To spell out this line of reasoning in slightly more detail, it may be recalled that little more than half a century ago, atoms were conceived as hard indivisible specks of solid matter of some ninety different varieties, the chemical elements. This notion was shattered by the discovery of X-rays and then of radium, an element that disintegrates spontaneously with emission of radiation, transmuting itself into a succession of radioactive elements and eventually turning into an isotope of lead. This was followed by the discovery that the stable elements are not unique species, but each consists of a mixture of isotopes, chemically identical but differing in atomic weight. The inference that atoms must be complex divisible entities was aided by the study of radiations and their interactions with matter. Surprisingly it appeared that the supposedly solid atoms consisted mainly of empty space, inhabited by very much smaller elementary particles. These were named initially as a heavy nucleus and light electrons whirling around in orbits, like the planets round the sun. Later the nucleus was shown to be complex also, containing neutrons and protons; gradually the new science of atomic physics has found it necessary to postulate a whole range of subatomic particles, their number having risen now to around 100.

Thus the essential characteristics of matter have been pushed right out of the physical world as we once thought of it, namely as hard solid reliable substance, the "hard core of existence." The "building blocks of the universe," as atoms were once called, are now conceived as complex but stable vortical centers in a force field, their stability conferred not by solidity but by a kind of rigidity arising from relationships of mutual attraction between these centers. So within a few decades physics has, so to speak, dematerialized matter into a tenuous condition, a force field that may well be considered akin to thought. The elementary particles turned out to be extraordinarily elusive shadowy entities. The electron, for example, does not behave at all like a little ball would do according to classical physics, having clearly definable position and velocity. On the contrary, when we can specify the speed of an electron, we cannot tell where it is with any precision; when we do know the position, then in turn its velocity becomes indeterminate. This is a simplified statement of Heisenberg's Uncertainty Principle. With the advent of the science of quantum mechanics, still stranger properties had to be attributed to the electron. In some circumstances it undoubtedly does behave as a particle; for example, when an electron and a positron (or antielectron) meet head-on, they annihilate each other and disappear in a burst of radiation. Yet under other circumstances electrons behave as bundles of wave forms, exhibiting interference phenomena, for instance, just like light waves. The electron "is at once a corpuscle and a wave"—a situation classified by Bohr as the Principle of Complementarity. As Heisenberg explained it:

> The concept of complementarity is meant to describe a situation in which we can look at one and the same event through two different frames of reference. These two frames mutually exclude each other, and only the juxtaposition of these contradictory frames provides an exhaustive view of the appearance of the phenomenon.

And, on another occasion:

> What the Copenhagen School calls complementarity accords
> very neatly with the Cartesian dualism of matter and mind.[4]

So at the heart of the physical world we find the electron,
which is unquestionably a single entity yet which displays
a striking dualism in its behavior. It is not surprising that
this situation has led some physicists to wonder about the
fundamental dualisms of mind and body, of spirit and
matter, that have plagued philosophers down the centuries. Could they be resolved into unities, by analogy with
the dualistic electron which is nevertheless a unity? Certainly this is a highly suggestive analogy; but what if it represents a general law of nature? As Wolfgang Pauli remarked at an earlier date:

> The general problem of the relationship between mind and
> body, between the inward and the outward, cannot be said to
> have been solved by the concept of psycho-physical parallel-
> ism postulated in the last century. Modern science has perhaps
> brought us nearer to a more satisfactory understanding of this
> relationship, by introducing the concept of complementarity
> into physics itself. It would be the more satisfactory solution if
> mind and body could be interpreted as complementary aspects
> of the same reality.[4]

Perhaps the entire objective and subjective worlds are not
entirely separate, as they seem, but are joined in one single
reality which appears to us as objective or subjective when
seen from different limited viewpoints. Cosmic Intelligence and the material world should perhaps be regarded as
aspects of one all-embracing unity, like the face and ob-
verse of a medal. What we sometimes call Spirit would be
Matter viewed from below, while correspondingly Matter
would be Spirit viewed from above, so to speak. Such
similies are poetic expressions not to be taken literally.
There are indeed no literal words for these mysteries, which
cannot be resolved intellectually. Taking account of the
support given by atomic physics, those who dislike philosophical dualities may like to meditate on the idea that all
such dualities may be subsumed within a more fundamental unity. If it can indeed by accepted that in some sense

Cosmic Intelligence and the material world comprise a unity, then we are back to the conclusion reached earlier that the universe is pervaded by intelligence.

The Coming of Man

The brief recapitulation of the story of evolution in Section Three was deliberately interrupted at the point before man appears on the scene, because he injects a completely new element into the process. Throughout the course of evolution in the plant and animal kingdoms, Cosmic Intelligence met no active opposition to its purpose. The only opposition was that imposed by the limited plasticity of the natural world, its inertial resistance to change. So progress was assured, though it was slow and jerky; it seemed to be marked by evolutionary experiments that failed, or that fulfilled a limited purpose before a species died out to make way for something superior, an entity better adapted for survival.

A new situation arose when man emerged and developed an independent mind as his chief attribute. Man then seized the power to choose for himself; he could elect to go along with the evolutionary tide or to oppose it. History shows that in fact he has often banded with his fellows to secure short-term advantage at the expense of weaker members of the human race. Perhaps the disastrous strife that has ensued from time to time has been necessary to sharpen his intelligence and bring him to realize his errors. Our reason, our intuition, and our sense of justice join with religion to proclaim that no section of mankind can achieve lasting happiness and prosperity until the whole of mankind is free to share it. Nevertheless most of us remain deaf to these exhortations, because our overriding concern is to retain the material advantages that the developed nations have secured for themselves. How will it all end? Toward what goal have aeons of struggle been directed? In what directions should man turn his own freely selected effort now?

Unity of Man and Nature

Though man now stands at the apex of the evolutionary

process, he remains intimately linked with all that has gone before. Unity is not just a pious hope but a scientific fact at every level. Already we are one with every other, and we are one with nature, though we seldom pause to recognize these things. At the physical level we share one earth: the atoms of our bodies are constantly changing, and with every breath we take in myriads of atoms previously used by others. It is said that most Englishmen have in their bodies a few atoms that once were Shakespeare's.

At the chemical level we share one pattern of metabolism: the thousands of chemical reactions, by which we digest our food and maintain our flesh and organs, are mostly common to all the animal kingdom and, in fact, plants use many of these same reactions along with others. It has thus become clear that throughout nature metabolic pathways are like a single theme with variations.

At the biological level we share one life: the evolutionary progress of living organisms is like an imposing design of branching stairways, and at no point is the step high enough for any denial of continuity. Individual cells in our bodies resemble lowly unicellular organisms; in embryonic life, too, many of the earilier forms are recapitulated.

At the social level we share one humanity: we are one social species with minor variations, and the history of civilization concerns our efforts at harmonious integration of increasingly large groups.

Finally, at the spiritual level we share one Cosmic Intelligence, one God, as some would say. For many this is no more than an article of religious acceptance, but for some it is a luminous certainty born of deep personal experience. When it is thus for all of us we shall no longer need to remind ourselves of these truths, and we shall be truly civilized. So man carries within himself the essence of all that has been and is now; and he has the power to build the future as he will.

The Road for Humanity

Man's intelligence can be his undoing or his salvation. Allied to his baser nature it leads to selfish antisocial behavior; allied to his spiritual qualities it leads toward cooperation, altruism, and unity. The human kingdom has evolved values other than those of mere survival in competition with others. Our highest impulses have no biological survival value; in fact they are the exact opposite in their consequences. This is a new phenomenon, a new factor in evolution. Such a mutation, expressing a purposeful spiritual and altruistic drive, is something entirely new in the evolutionary pattern of material forms. Altruistic behavior may indeed lack survival value in the strictly biological sense, but survival value it certainly does have, in the wider context of human civilization. Doubtless we shall continue to falter, but clearly this is the path we must take. In the long run, indeed, it will be perilous not to do so. We have gone a long way already, and by now we know too much to turn back.

The ideas are abroad and are gaining more and more adherents as insight dawns, bringing something akin to religious conversion, but one in which reason and faith are allied. Good works in abundance are also demanded if the world's ills are to be healed before it is too late, for it will be an exceedingly complex task to extricate ourselves voluntarily from entrenched positions. However, it is encouraging that influential groups in many countries are now actively working on the problems.

It is a hard road that humanity has chosen and, unless we keep faith, the human race may exterminate itself. But so long as we can avoid this ultimate disaster, there is no desperate urgency. On a geological time scale, human civilization is extremely young. So, provided we contrive to move steadily forward in the right direction, then presumably there are millions of years before us as a race in which to achieve the perfection we seek. It must be emphasized again that this is not just wishful thinking but a strictly scientific assessment of human possibilities.

As time passes and progress along the true road continues, considerate, harmonious activity should gain prominence in personal and national affairs and it will then be seen to embody its own unique satisfaction, the realization that it brings the spiritual benison of integration of all one's faculties and their realignment with Cosmic Intelligence. The necessary material sacrifices may come to be regarded as willing contributions, just as in simpler times men joyously paid their tithes to the Church. This may seem an unrealistic Utopian idea, but nothing less can save mankind from ultimate disaster. It could unite those who profess to be religious with others who have little use for churches—the foundation perhaps of a New Crusade.

This is a challenge. But it is also a tremendously hopeful outlook, which contrasts strongly with the gloomy forebodings current in some circles today.

REFERENCES

[1]V.A. Firsoff, *Life, Mind and Galaxies,* Oliver and Boyd, Edinburgh and London, 1967, 102.

[2]E. Schrödinger, *What is Life?* Cambridge University Press, 1967.

[3]Bhagavad Gita, translated by Annie Besant (Krishna speaking at the end of the Tenth Discourse).

[4]W. Heisenberg; W. Pauli, quoted by A. Koestler in *The Roots of Coincidence,* Hutchinson, London, 1972.